LONDON SOUTH EAST COLLEGES

ORPINGTON

Learning Centre

Late return of this item will be charged at 10p per day

Items can be renewed in person,
by email: Orpingtonlrc@lsec.ac.uk or
by phone: 020 3954 5002

You are responsible for this item; if unreturned, lost or damaged you will need to pay for the replacement.

First published 1996
Reprinted 2008

PCCS BOOKS Ltd
2 Cropper Row
Alton Road
Ross-on-Wye
Herefordshire
HR9 5LA
UK
Tel +44 (0)1989 763 900
contact@pccs-books.co.uk
www.pccs-books.co.uk

© Anne Kearney 1996

**Counselling, Class and Politics:
Undeclared influences in therapy**

British Library Cataloguing in Publication Data
A catalogue record for this book is available
from the British Library

ISBN 978 1 898 05909 7

Printed by CPod, Cromwell Press, Trowbridge, UK

Contents

For J.M.

Introduction

This book has been written as much to clarify ideas for myself as to communicate those to others, and as I wrote it I became aware of where my confusion and uncertainties lie. The book arose out of my own feelings of unease about my own politics and my role as a counsellor. I originally trained as a social scientist and spent many years teaching and developing courses for adults who came back into education wanting to improve their lives as well as those of their children. It was my role, as I saw it, to facilitate that.

My counselling training was marked for me by great personal development, greater awareness of the role I wanted to play in relation to people and, as such, it was very challenging and demanding. It was also, however, deeply unsatisfying in that there were huge gaps in areas of awareness and knowledge which I felt were crucial to me personally and to my intellectual and emotional development generally.

I have been a socialist of a kind for many years and some of the ideas I was exposed to in training seemed to me to 'fit' exactly with the kinds of ideas I had been excited by in my twenties and continue to be excited by in my fifties—the possibility of things being other than they are; the attempt to move away from others' judgements to an 'internal locus of evaluation'; the opportunity to feel and be respected by others and to respect them in return; the equal valuing of all human beings and so on.

I felt at home with these ideas then and still do, but I kept expecting something else in my training, some challenges to the political ideas which inhibit the organismic self from gaining acceptance, some acknowledgement that, as counsellors, we cannot afford to allow ourselves to be imbued with the conventional wisdom of our times, which pits individual against individual, decries compassion and fails to draw attention to the damaging social, as well as personal, environment in which many people live.

I felt frustrated and let down by the absence of political challenges in my training and still do. There was all the potential in the counselling literature and in counselling training to make what I see as the necessary political links, yet somehow they were never made. I became self-conscious as a trainee about always 'harping on' about politics, and I became anxious about alienating trainers and other trainees. The temptation was to ignore my concerns and my unease and on many occasions I did just that, though whenever I did I felt bad about it afterwards.

The concerns I felt then have if anything increased, so this is my attempt to do what I can to redress what I believe to be a gap in counselling training and counselling awareness in general.

I have no intention in this book of trying to convert readers to any particular political position but I do have every intention of trying to persuade readers to the view that politics and political ideas matter in counselling. I am convinced that they matter at every level of counselling, from training to seeing clients, from BACP regulations to supervision, and I am also convinced that we do less than justice to ourselves as counsellors and to our clients if we do not face the challenges this presents us with.

I know that there are many counsellors out there with much more experience of some of the issues addressed here than I have and I feel a certain measure of 'cheekiness' in going against some of their ideas. However, I'm going to do it anyway!

I decided not to write this in an academic style with referencing etc., since my primary aim is to make the ideas accessible and I found that I could better explore the ideas if I reduced them to their essentials.

I want to thank my friends and colleagues Pauline Edwards and Ann Roberts. Ann for word processing my dreadful handwriting and supporting and encouraging me; Pauline for listening to me expounding ideas, calming my anxieties about deadlines and generally being a friend and sounding board. I want also to thank Martin for his help in the word-processing marathon.

Anne Kearney
Manchester
June 1996

Chapter 1

Counselling and Ideology

Government ... is about stability. Keeping things going, preventing anarchy, stopping society falling to bits ... Still being here tomorrow ... Government isn't about good and evil, it's only about order and chaos. (*Yes, Minister,* Volume 3, by Jonathan Lynn and Anthony Jay, 1983, p. 116)

> **Overview**
> In this chapter I want to:
> • explore the notion of ideology,
> • refer to the ideology connected with counselling,
> • look at some of the challenges made by some writers to that ideology – especially those which look at the effects of racism and sexism on our practise as counsellors, and
> • present my own concerns about the challenge that issues of class make to counselling ideology.

The term 'ideology' has a slightly tarnished image; it is often used as a term of abuse to refer to some set of beliefs and values which we ourselves do not share, and which we 'accuse' someone else of having. But there is an important clue here about its real meaning – ideology is in some way about what people believe and what is important to them. An ideology, then, is a set of beliefs and values which we hold knowingly – and sometimes, not knowingly. I may know, for instance, that I have a set of beliefs about family life, or the importance of work in people's lives, and those beliefs will be consistent with how I value family life and work. I may have other sets of values that I am less aware of.

Generally, then, an ideology is any system of ideas which underlies any social and political action. This definition sees ideology as relative – it refers to *any* system of ideas, whatever subject it is applied to. In political debate, the term ideology often has negative connotations; this is evident in party politics when, for example, each side accuses the other of supporting or not supporting privatisation, for ideological reasons. Used in this way, the suggestion is that there is something pretty bad about taking a position 'for ideological reasons'.

In its present-day use, the term ideology seems to refer to any system of ideas that justifies the subordination of one group by another; so we read about 'white ideology', or 'male ideology', meaning that the ideology is biased, partisan and not, therefore, 'true or neutral'.

Consider

In small groups discuss what you believe to be the ideology of any *organisation* in which you have worked.

Look, for example, at any documentation of *religious beliefs* and see if you can identify its ideology.

Take some activity such as *parenting*, or *being a partner*, and brainstorm any ideology that you connect with it.

In each case see if you can identify any group which is disadvantaged by the ideology and any which benefits from it.

Can clients be harmed by our ideologies?

I suggest that almost everything we do is justified by some ideological set of ideas, and that counselling as an activity is no exception to this. I also suggest that one of the reasons why the ideology of counselling is not always apparent to us is that we cannot easily accept that the activities, beliefs and values of counselling may have consequences for some clients which are other than we intend. In other words, it is difficult for us as counsellors to believe that the ideology of counselling may lead to justifying the subordination of some clients, when what we intend is exactly the opposite. We intend, I believe genuinely, that the process of counselling/therapy will result in the empowerment of clients, not their subordination. Yet recent developments in counselling have very broadly hinted at the former possibility, though not using the same terms as I am. Books on the importance of race and gender issues in counselling, and the dangers which may result for the client when we ignore these issues, are all part of our general concern that counselling really is safe and empowering.

These concerns have appeared relatively late in counselling books in comparison with other areas of study. In education, for instance, debates about issues of race and gender appeared on the agenda at a much earlier stage and greater awareness of these became part of teacher education as long ago as the sixties and seventies. The 1944 Butler Education Acts, for example, recognised the bias in the education system which prevented working-class children from receiving opportunities to develop their talents and to enter the higher education system at no financial cost.

Issues of discrimination and the possible impact of gender and race now have an accepted role in the training of counsellors and obviously this represents great progress. Awareness has grown mainly through considering and extending the notion of a power imbalance in the counselling relationship itself. Counsellors have always recognised that their role in relation to their clients is not one of equality and not just because there is a danger that the client may put them in the role of 'the expert'.

Consider
- In what ways may clients perceive the counsellor as more powerful and why?
- What do you believe counsellors may do to either challenge or reinforce power inequalities?

I believe that the ideology of counselling was challenged by the recognition that gender and race issues are an intrinsic part of the counselling relationship and cannot be ignored. I believe that up to that point most counsellors felt their ideological beliefs were such that (provided they remained aware of the power imbalance at the centre of the counselling relationship) they could be pretty sure that counselling would empower clients – all other things being equal.

This set of beliefs has two component parts. One is theoretical and derives from the study of the therapeutic theories the counsellor has learned. These theories (and of course they vary in the concepts they use and how they describe and explain the therapeutic process) describe how to create and sustain the conditions that facilitate the client in taking charge of their life. The second component is much less specific, and much less acknowledged by counsellors. It is often more like a set of assumptions than the first component; assumptions about being non-judgemental, not allowing the counsellor/therapist personal prejudices or social prejudices to intervene in the counselling process.

It was that second component which was challenged by the criticisms of mainstream practice, put forward by feminist counsellors and transcultural counsellors who asserted that 'neutral' attitudes claimed by 'mainstream' counsellors were, in fact, far from neutral, and certainly not neutral in their consequences for female clients and clients from different cultural backgrounds than their counsellors.

Feminist counsellors took the view that, as with most other professions, counselling is based largely on a set of assumptions which are predominantly male. Counselling incorporates taken-for-granted male assumptions about the division of roles between women and men; it is based mainly on male theories of the personality development of males, which are then generalised to females; it takes the unequal distribution of power between women and men in society as 'given'; and it is derived from linear systems of thinking and reasoning which may not be an accurate description of how women think and reason. Non-feminist counsellors, the argument went, may well reinforce gender-based power differences and (unwittingly) coerce female clients into adopting and accepting traditional roles which may have created their difficulties and distress in the first place.

Much of the substance of these arguments has been accepted by many counsellors, and forms part of most good training courses. I do not want, however, to exaggerate the acceptability of these claims either by counsellors, trainers or indeed, trainees. My personal experience suggests (though, of course, I have no means of knowing how representative these experiences are) that many trainees see these arguments as unacceptable, not because they are unconvinced by them, but because they see them as non-neutral – in other words, as political. As such, they feel they are inappropriate in what is an otherwise 'politically neutral' activity.

> **Consider**
> • What do you feel as you read the summary above?
>   • Do you feel that it is important to discuss the ideas
>   contained in the summary, and if so, why?
>
> • If you had to persuade somebody who was opposed to these
>   ideas to at least consider them, how might you go about it?

As we can see, there is a claim being made that there is, indeed, a male ideology, one which is so pervasive that many men resist the idea that it exists at all. Many women, too, so take for granted the dominance of this ideology that they may feel themselves denying its existence or, where this is conceded, denying that it has any implications of making women's ideology subordinate. My suggestion here is that the danger for clients of our insisting on our gender neutrality does not remove the consequences of non-neutrality.

The arguments made in relation to transcultural counselling are obviously different in detail but very similar in structure. There exists, it is argued, a white ideology: an ideology of dominance which can be denied by those who believe it precisely because it is so pervasive in countries like Britain that it is completely taken for granted. Like other ideologies, it appears not to be merely a relative set of beliefs about the world but a 'set of facts' so self-evident that it never needs to be made explicit, and therefore never needs to be justified by evidence or argument. Part of this ideology is a set of assumptions about people who are black or Asian or from other minority ethnic communities. White ideology, the argument suggests, implies that norms and values, expectations and beliefs (which are actually *culturally relative*) are *universal*, therefore they can be used (often 'out of awareness') as a benchmark against which the norms, values and beliefs of other groups can be perceived as deficient in some sense.

This obviously can have devastating implications for individual clients from communities and cultures other than that of the dominant white culture.

> **Consider**
> Brainstorm in the whole group, see if you can come up with some of the effects on black people of being assessed (formally or otherwise) by a representative of the dominant white group.
>
> Divide into pairs and consider some of the practical ways in which some of those effects might be prevented.

Counselling, ideology and disability

A third set of arguments claiming the non-neutrality of counsellors, and the existence of a particular ideology, has come from groups of disabled people. Their arguments obviously vary in focus but, basically, the claim is being made that in training courses, in physical and practical ways, disabled people are frequently, in effect, excluded, and not only by the physical impairments they deal with in a built environment planned and organised by non-disabled people: some people with a disability argue that counsellors continue to operate with a medical model of the world and attribute all the difficulties disabled people experience to their impairments. In reality it is a set of ideological beliefs about impairment which is the disabling process and, to the extent that counsellors fail to challenge that ideology, they are part of the process which disempowers people with a disability. Simple things like always designing training exercises which offer a range of ways of achieving a learning goal – some involving physical activities, some not – can ensure (whether there are people with a disability in the learning group or not) that perceptions of people with a disability as *disabled only by their impairment* can be challenged.

Many people with a disability perceive the failure of training groups to do this as a reluctance on the part of trainers to challenge their own (and trainees') ideological assumptions about disability and, to the extent that this is so, counselling training itself becomes part of the social process by which people become disabled.

Consider

Divide into small groups and design a small training exercise which does not exclude anybody from participating. State clearly the aims and objectives of your training exercise.

Develop a method of learning experientially in a group which is inclusive of everyone.

- What difficulties did you find in doing this, if any?
- Did it challenge any assumptions you might previously have made?

Apply the substance of the arguments I have been summarising to issues of sexual orientation. You could ask yourself some of the following questions:

- Is there a dominant ideology about sexual orientation? If so, state it simply and clearly.
- Does that ideology have implications for those who are gay or lesbian? If so, what are they?

Can you relate this to counselling practice? What issues, for instance, might a straight male counsellor need to be particularly aware of if he is counselling a lesbian woman or a gay man?

Counsellors as political beings

I have reviewed these arguments, however briefly (I hope without distorting them) because there is a set of arguments I want to put forward which is, in many respects, generally similar to the claims I have described.

I suggest that the claims made about white ideology, about gender ideology, and about the ideology of 'non-people' with a disability, all cast doubts on the neutrality of counsellors and, by implication, on the process of counselling. In addition I suggest that counsellors are, like everyone else, political beings with a political ideology (of which they may not be aware) which has direct and indirect consequences for clients. I want to raise the issue that counselling is informed by a set political values and beliefs which are part of the dominant political ideology of the society in which counselling is being practised.

In this book I will argue that the issue of class is almost never referred to in counselling at any level – in training courses, in training manuals, or in books about counselling – and I believe that our failure to take account of class really matters.

Consider

In a large group to see what words you come up with to describe 'class'.

- What ideas do you associate with the word 'class'?

Work in pairs, and describe to your partner the characteristics you associate with class. Swap over. Make no judgements about your or your partner's contribution, just note them.

Consider

Look at the checklist below and see whether you can divide it into the sorts of things different classes of people do. Use just two groups, working-class people, and people from other groups. Just take a general view, there will always be exceptions.

1. Go on package holidays.
2. Shop at Waitrose.
3. Send their children to public schools.
4. Play bowls.
5. Speak a second language.
6. Live in a detached house.
7. Go sailing.
8. Play in a darts team.
9. Vote for the Green Party.
10. Buy clothes at the local market.
11. Buy toys at Christmas from a catalogue.
12. Interested in gardening.
13. Go bird-watching.
14. Listen to the local radio station.
15. Have plain carpets in their house.
16. Go the opera.
17. Leave school as early as possible.
18. Attend church regularly.
19. Have a degree.
20. Smoke.

21. Belong to one of the professions.
22. Listen to Radio 4.
23. Keep pigeons as a hobby.
24. Have an allotment.
25. Read the Guardian.
26. Live in a council house.
27. Develop illnesses connected with the kind of work they do.
28. Eat vegetarian food.
29. Live near their relations.
30. Work shifts.
31. Trainer on a counselling course.

When you've done your checklist it might be interesting to compare your answers with a partner and see where you have agreed and where you have differed.

• Can you draw any conclusions from this activity?

Consider

Two people remain in the room while the rest go outside. The two people decide how the group outside is to be divided. It could be that anyone who has brown eyes belongs to one group, anyone who has any other eye colour belongs to another group.

The group outside is not told how they have been divided. Instead, the whole group is given a topic to discuss with the two people who remained inside as facilitators. Any opinion expressed by the brown-eyed people is treated with respect: they are deferred to; when sweets or coffee are dispensed they are given more than the others in the group, and they are asked by the facilitators to decide when to have a break and for how long.

• How long does it take for the group to recognise which members are in the 'favoured' group?

• How do they begin to recognise on what basis the 'favoured' group are 'a group'?

• What did you learn about 'class' from this exercise?

These class differences, I suggest, are not merely 'equal but different'; they involve huge disparities of income, wealth, power and status, which are so taken for granted that we fail to take account of their impact on every aspect of our lives and those of our clients.

The social differences between groups also represent different 'ways of being', different attitudes, different aspirations, a different sense of identity and so on, in almost every sphere of our lives.

My intention here is to convince you that class is very important in our lives and that there is some level at which we know this and recognise that, as well as there being individual differences between people, there are also other group differences: differences which derive from the social section of society to which we belong.

Chapter 2

Social Stratification

Overview
This chapter introduces:
- the idea of stratification by which people in a society are divided into groups,
- the different types of stratification,
- social class as a form of stratification system, and
- the impact class has on counselling.

The stratification system which exists in present-day Western societies is that of social class. People are divided into social groups, according to some writers, on the basis of what kind of work they do, or according to others their 'relationship to the means of production' (that is whether they own the capital, plant, equipment and factories, or work for a wage).

Social class is a relatively open system of stratification in which there are no legal or religious constraints on moving from one social class to another. This movement is known as social mobility and often measured by comparing the occupation of parents (usually fathers!) with that of their children.

Consider
Try this as an exercise in your group. Ask each person to state the occupation of their parent(s) and compare it with their own.

- How much social mobility has there been in your group?

British society has not always been based on class as a principle of stratification. From the Middle Ages until the Industrial Revolution British society was organised around the feudal system, the basis of which was land as the main source of wealth, power and prestige.

Most of what we hear about this system comes from the Doomsday Book which was, in effect, a census made by William I (1066–1087).

Nominally, all the land in England belonged to King William but, in reality, chief nobles and churchmen received parcels of land in return for their services to him. In particular, they advised him on his council and they provided knights and soldiers for his army. To do this, the nobles and churchmen divided their land amongst lesser tenants, particularly knights, who, in exchange, committed themselves to the military service of the King. The knights in turn divided their land amongst peasant farmers, of whom there were two types: freemen and serfs (who made up the vast majority of the population).

Serfs did not have freedom of movement; they swore oaths of allegiance to their lord and they farmed the land, withholding only part of the crop for themselves, the remainder being the 'due of the lord'. Serfs had the right to graze cattle on common lands as well as the right to be protected by their lords.

Consider

It is interesting to compare the system of serfdom to slavery. Try answering the following questions:

- How is this system different from a system of slavery?

- What rights and obligations did a slave owner have in relation to his slaves?

- What rights and obligations did a slave have in relation to his owner?

The Indian caste system

Other societies are stratified in a quite different way from either a feudal or a class system. One example of this is the caste system of India, which has existed for thousands of years. Though the influence of the caste system has declined to some extent as India has industrialised, it nevertheless still retains great importance in the lives of people, both amongst Indian people living in India and amongst Hindu communities living in Britain.

The caste system is based around a set of beliefs and values,

Hinduism, which provides support for this type of stratification. A caste is made up of families who share a common family name and who perceive themselves to be the descendants of a common ancestor. Each caste is sub-divided into 'Jatis', each of which specialises in a particular occupation, for instance, porters, builders, goldsmiths, etc. The individual is born into a caste and remains in that caste for life, that is, the position of each person in the caste system is ascribed from birth. People marry within their caste.

The castes form a hierarchy based on the notion of religious purity; those at the top being perceived as clean and pure whilst those at the bottom are perceived as unclean and impure. The 'lower' castes are responsible for unclean tasks such as disposing of dead animals or human waste; tasks which those higher up the caste system would regard as degrading and defiling. Contact between the castes is extremely limited and ritualised. In extreme cases, in South India for instance, members of the higher castes would call out as they walk along the road so that people from the lowest classes would get out of their way and not pollute the air the higher castes breathe.

The Brahmin form the highest caste – these are holy men whose wealth, status and power come from the fact that they are perceived to be very pure in religious terms.

The Kshatriya is a kind of royal family and is the second-highest ranking caste, the caste of warriors and kings. They were the rulers and their duty was one of protection of the people.

The third is Vaisya, the merchants and farmers, and the fourth, Sudra, is the worker caste, whose destiny is to serve the higher castes. Sudras, although essential, are treated as lower-class citizens, getting the lowest paid jobs and living in the poorest areas. Poverty is prevalent, but education is not, the majority being illiterate.

People who belong to the fourth caste are those such as teachers, weavers or barbers who serve the two castes above them and are not regarded as being a polluting agent by those higher up the caste system than themselves.

At the base of the pyramid which represents the caste system are the Untouchables who, as mainly manual workers, are despised by the Brahmin and other higher castes and often live in segregated huts outside villages or even in the middle of rice fields where they cannot pollute people from other castes.

Consider
- Are there any similarities that you can see between the caste system and the class system?

- What seem to you to be the main differences between the two?

- Imagine a completely new system of stratification. What might be the principles upon which stratification is based? It could be height or weight, eye colour or anything else you decide upon.

- What sorts of beliefs/ideology do you think would need to exist in order to justify it?

- How do you think these beliefs might be passed on to the younger generation?

- What might happen to individuals who refused to accept the ideology?

Class in present-day Britain

I have said that I think social class is the main system of stratification in Britain, although there is no generally accepted way of defining class. Some people who research in this field use job or occupation as the main index of class division, some use status or the prestige of a person's job to identify class position.

The Registrar General's social class stratification is used for official purposes when the government commissions reports or surveys. This system is widely used (with modifications) by advertisers who may want to use 'niche marketing' techniques to target a particular income group. It is a classification which allocates or assigns particular jobs to particular classes on the basis of 'the general standing within the community' (quite what is meant by 'general standing' is difficult to be sure about).

The classification divides jobs into two general categories: middle class and working class, and then subdivides each class as shown in the table below. You may be familiar with some of the categories used from newspaper reports or television programmes.

The Registrar General's social classification		
Social Class		**Examples of occupations in each class**
Middle Class	Class 1 Professional	Accountant, doctor, dentist, solicitor, university lecturer.
	Class 2 Managerial and technical	Manager, teacher, librarian, nurse, farmer.
	Class 3 (Non-manual) Clerical and minor supervisory	Clerk, shop assistant, policeman, draughtsman, sales representative.
Working Class	Class 3 (Manual) Skilled manual	Electrician, tailor, bus driver, printer, cook.
	Class 4 Semi-skilled manual	Agricultural worker, postman, telephone operator, fisherman, barman.
	Class 5 Unskilled manual	Railway porter, labourer, lorry driver's mate, window cleaner, office cleaner.

Consider

Ideas and systems of social classification are not arbitrary or neutral.

- If you as a group were assigning these jobs within a classification system, would you evaluate them in the same way?

You could cut out strips of paper, each one with a job written on it. Then within your group, work with a partner and classify the jobs in a hierarchy.

Compare your classification system with another pair of group members.

- Did your evaluation and classification agree?

- What, if any, were your areas of disagreement?

- How do you, as a whole group, think that disagreements in classification might arise?

While the Registrar General identifies the existence of five main social groups based on occupation, other social observers and theorists disagree. Karl Marx (1818–1883) gives a very different view of the class system and one which is still very influential.

He identifies only two classes: the ruling class (which he calls the bourgeoisie) and the subject class (which he calls the proletariat). The ruling class, he claims, is numerically very small and incredibly powerful. The proletariat (or working class) is the largest group by far including, as it does, everyone who is not a member of the bourgeoisie.

The ruling class has, according to Marx's view, vast amounts of power, disproportionate to its size, which it derives from owning 'the means of production'. By this he means (in an industrial society) the capital, the factories, the machinery and the raw materials used for production. In agricultural societies the 'means of production' would be land, and the ruling class would be those who own the land.

The working class, on the hand, own little besides their skills and their willingness to work for the ruling class in return for a wage.

Marx claimed that the ruling class is non-productive in the sense that as a class it does not actually produce anything. What is produced in terms of manufactured goods and services is generated by the labour of the working class. The wealth this produces is then taken away from them in the form of profits for the ruling class.

Consider

There are several differences between the two systems of social classification and these give rise to very different understandings of class.

- What are the main differences between Marx's idea of class and that of the Registrar General?

Marx is saying that the ruling class have a monopoly of economic power, but he is claiming two other things as well: that as a result of their monopoly of economic power, the ruling class acquire two other monopolies:

1. a monopoly of political power,
2. a monopoly of 'ideas' (by which he means ideology).

He claims that the relationship between the two main classes is characterised by inequalities and the exploitation of one by another. We can see this more clearly, perhaps, by looking some more at what Marx means by 'a monopoly of ideas'. He is pointing out that the working class are constantly exploited, politically and economically, by a small minority of people who share a set of norms, values and beliefs which justify that exploitation. Why should this be allowed by the working class to persist? The answer, he claims, lies in the fact that the ruling class *do* have an ideology which legitimates and justifies the inequalities from which they benefit, and this ideology is imposed upon and then internalised by the working class. In other words, working class people themselves begin to legitimise and justify the inequalities of the class system by absorbing and believing ruling class ideology (Marx calls this 'false consciousness') or by simply failing to recognise it, because it appears so ordinary, familiar and therefore unchallengeable.

Acceptance of social inequality is, according to present day Marxists, 'part of the air we breathe' to the extent that, like goldfish living in a bowl, the last thing we would recognise as being all around us is water.

Furthermore, learning to remain unaware of social inequalities or to accept them as 'normal' and inevitable is facilitated by various agencies such as the state (children in our education system are not even taught that they live in a capitalist system, never mind being taught about the inequalities capitalism produces). Marxists argue that the main purposes of the education system have little to do with the realisation of each child's talents and abilities. They have much to do with indoctrination into acceptance of the inequalities of capitalism and the preparation of the younger generation to become the next labour force who can be relied on not to question their own exploitation or possibly even to recognise it.

As well as indoctrination into acceptance of ruling class ideology, Marxists argue that there are a number of 'social control' mechanisms which can be mobilised to coerce and/or persuade people to conform even when they do not accept the ideology. One of these is to label people troublemakers, paranoid, having a chip on their shoulder, fanatics or extremists. In many cases, for instance in the earlier stages of industrialisation, workers were forbidden by the Combination Acts to form trade unions and thereby prevented from persuading other workers to challenge the power of the employers. It is less uncommon than we might think for workers seen as troublemakers to be put on a list of undesirables and therefore jobless, unable to support their families. Other social controls Marxists claim, may be less in the form of punishment for not conforming than in reward for doing so, by promotion or increases in wages.

I am aware that some of these ideas may seem extreme, unfamiliar and possibly little to do with counselling. But I believe there are strong parallels with counselling, and to try and illustrate this I would like to make some connections. We may accept the Registrar General's view of class (which portrays society as a kind of ladder with the most prestigious, powerful and well-paid jobs at the top, descending to groupings of people who do the less prestigious, less powerful, less well-paid jobs at the bottom), or a Marxist view of class, which portrays class in horizontal terms with one class at one extreme, holding a monopoly of wealth, power and ideology, and the working class at the other extreme, holding none of these. Which of these views most appeals to us is probably a matter of personal preference and personal experience. My argument does not rest on holding one view of this rather than the other. My claim is that (to different degrees) *in either case* social inequalities are agreed to exist and *in either case* there is some degree of acceptance ideologically of these inequalities *whether we are aware of it or not*.

The suggestion I am making here is that there is a connection between the ideology that prevails in an unequal society and how we as individuals and groups are positioned in an unequal system. The more powerful the group to which we belong the less likely, generally, we are to question the system which legitimises and confers these privileges.

I am not suggesting that it is impossible to be a member of a socially powerful group and to question the system which confers those powers, simply that it is not very common for that to be the case, and that most people remain unaware of the political, economic and social processes which form the scaffolding of their lives. Most of us, most of the time, I believe, take the framework within which we live and the ideology that justifies it as a 'given' and rarely challenge, question or even become aware of it.

There are similarities here with being a child in a family setting. We take the framework, the assumptions, the roles and the ideology of our particular family as 'given', they are just 'how things are done'. Not until we are a bit older or see how other families operate do we realise that our way is 'a' way of doing things, not 'the' way. In other words the framework of our family life is often not apparent to us until we step outside it and see it in all its relativity.

The same thing applies to broader cultural frameworks: they are often not even perceived because they create the order and the meaning-structure of our lives.

In each of these examples, what we are also taking as a 'given' is the distribution of power as it takes place in our society both because it is seen as 'given' and because we (if we are members of a relatively powerful group) have a vested interest in *not* recognising and/or challenging power inequalities.

Even when this is not so, I believe that many counsellors (and people generally) tend to believe, and often claim, that they are 'not political'. They may mean by this that they do not have a strong preference for one party over another, or they are not politically active in their community, or they do not (and are not interested in) discussing politics or reading about politics. They may see themselves as 'apolitical'. And this is another meaning: that the person espouses no political ideology, no particular view of the world. But I believe that having no political ideology of which we are aware *is not at all the same thing* as not having any political ideology. On the contrary, our 'unaware' ideology seems to me to be the most potentially influential ideology as far as clients are concerned. This is so, I believe, because:

a) Anything that we as counsellors allow to be unexamined (like our sexism or racism, etc.) is much more likely to influence our relationship with a client than something we become, and remain, aware of.

b) A major reason for believing ourselves to have no ideology could be that this is an accurate reflection of the ideology dominant in our culture/class etc. and, as such, taken for granted and never challenged. That ideology, to the extent to which it *does* reflect current external and dominant beliefs will be hierarchical, individualistic, involve notions of self-interest and competitiveness as 'natural' and 'normal': beliefs which may well be damaging to some clients.

I do not believe that it is possible to operate in the world without an ideology, without a set of beliefs and values about the world which render it meaningful, comprehensible and orderly (as well as chaotic). Equally I do not believe that ideologies (*any* ideologies) are neutral in any sense. They are not neutral because they value some things, events, people over others; they categorise reality in certain ways and they 'rule in' certain possibilities and 'rule out' others.

Consider

Working in pairs see if, together with your partner you can produce three statements starting with the phase 'I believe that people are ...' Offer your statement to another pair and receive their statement.

• Can you identify any kind of ideological beliefs which are implicit in the statements you have received?

Chapter 3

Social Class and Counselling

Overview

I have been arguing that the class to which a client and a counsellor belong are (where they differ) often ignored in the literature on power inequalities in counselling. In this chapter I would like to examine and summarise some of the main differences between the social classes as indicated by research findings.

To begin, it might help you to look at your own experience of this by answering the questions in the box below:

Consider

On your own, describe who you see as belonging to your family. Compare your description with that of another person in your group.

- What did your description have (if anything) in common with the other person's description?

- Were any of the similarities or differences attributable to class?

Class and family structure

Research suggests, for instance, that many working-class families have a rather different structure from that of many middle-class families. The structure of traditional working-class families is often inter-generational or 'extended' including grandparents, uncles, aunts and cousins in close connection with each other, sometimes living very close to each other. The bond between a married daughter and her mother is typically very strong and they rely on each other a lot in both practical and emotional ways.

Amongst middle-class families, grandparents, uncles and aunts may play a different role – just as important, but different. Since it is very common for middle-class people to move away from where they were brought up, the family is often much more geographically scattered. So although there may still be strong emotional bonds between the generations sustained in spite of geographical distance, that particular kind of connection is different from the day-to-day intimacy and often mutual dependency which is still common in many working-class families.

Consider

Look at your experience of family life and consider how this might relate to counselling. Individually answer the following questions:

- How often do you have contact with one or both of your parents? With a sibling or nieces/nephews, if you have any?

- If you needed to borrow money who would you ask first?

Compare these patterns with others in your training group and see whether you can identify any of the differences as being related to the social class you belong to.

Discuss the following questions:

- What kinds of misunderstandings/difficulties might arise between a client who was brought up in a working-class family and whose partner is middle class?

- As a counsellor, why would it be important for you to be class-aware if a client told you about one or more of the difficulties you identified in your group?

Another important difference between the classes is that of marriage roles. There are two possible types of 'conjugal roles': the first (segregated roles) where there is a very clear division of work between the couple, the woman has authority over and is responsible for the physical and emotional well-being of everyone in the family while the man is the provider (and sometimes the one who metes out punishment too). In these relationships couples often spend their leisure time separately: the women with her friends and family, the man with his friends (not often with his family).

The second type of marriage roles are called 'joint conjugal roles' within which there is a much less rigid division of work between the genders; money tends to be handled jointly and decisions made jointly. There is greater sharing of authority and power within the relationship and companionship between the couple tends to be very highly valued.

Traditional working-class family life tends to centre around a couple (where it is not a lone parent heading the household) who have segregated roles, whilst middle-class couples have tended to have joint roles. (Interestingly, at the very top of the social hierarchy, conjugal roles tend to be very similar to those at the bottom!)

There are, of course, some exceptions to the generalisation, particularly where a working-class couple have moved away from the neighbourhood in which they have grown up. There is, too, a general *social* tendency for conjugal roles to become joint rather than segregated, but the general *class* difference is often still apparent.

Consider
- Why would it be helpful for a counsellor to be aware of these class differences in marriage styles?
- What assumptions might you as a counsellor make about the marriage roles of a client from a different class background from yourself?
- Why might these assumptions matter in terms of a client's process?

Language, gender, class and counselling

A major difference between the classes is claimed to be the different ways in which groups use language. Language is such a complex phenomenon that it is beyond the scope of this chapter to do more than look very simplistically and crudely at the social aspects of how we communicate with each other verbally. Nevertheless there are still some useful points to be examined.

Language is not a socially neutral means of communicating with each other; it is influenced by a whole range of social factors such as gender, age, race/ethnicity and many other variables. Gender differences in language use have been well researched, so we know that the differences between how men and women use language, for instance, directly reflect the power differences and social differences between women and men in society. Contrary to stereotypes, women speak less in mixed gender groups than men do and when women do speak they more often than not play a supporting role either to men or to other women in the group. We know that women use language much more concisely than men (we have to, we're given less 'listening space') and are generally less supported when speaking in mixed gender groups. When women speak, men less often ask questions to elicit more information, they give less verbal feedback and they comment less on what has been said.

Consider

This activity can be a good group exercise in training. Brainstorm and then discuss answers to the following questions:

- What implications might this have for a female client speaking to an unaware male counsellor?

- What feelings might a female client have about herself if a male counsellor reacts verbally as the research indicates many men do?

- What conclusions might a female client reach about the counsellor's level of interest in her?

- How might a female counsellor respond verbally to a male client compared with a female client?

- What might you conclude from the above about how verbal behaviour is connected to socially maintained power differences?

Women tend to use what are called 'tag questions' at the end of sentences, phrases such as 'isn't it?', 'don't you' and so on, in order to try to do two things: firstly, to ensure that they gain some feedback which they might not otherwise get and, secondly, to include the listener more actively in the conversation.

Consider

Work in pairs for this exercise, if possible. Allocate yourselves the titles 'A' and 'B'. A speaks for two minutes without any tag questions at the end of sentences, talking about any topic of his/her choice. Note what that felt like to each of you.

Now A speaks for two minutes, again on any topic, this time using tag questions. Notice how this feels for each of you.

Reverse the speak/listen roles and check the feelings again.

Not only is it the case that gender differences emerge in the ways we have identified; even more important differences emerge when we examine how each gender frames the content of what is being said. Tannen (1992), writing on linguistics suggests that the content of what is said between people is processed differently by men and women. This is clear from a simple thing like tag questions where, for women, the meaning of the phrase may be a seeking after connectedness, while for men it might be seeking status. This does not, of course, mean that women never seek status, or men connectedness; what it means is that the social roles imposed on women and men highlight status and connectedness differently and that this is reflected in how women and men frame communications. If, for example, I am chatting with a male friend and he tells me that he has made a decision to do such and such a thing and I (interested in his motives and maybe empathising with him) seeking connectedness ask 'Why have you decided that?', my friend may frame that question as a challenge to his decision and feel threatened. In other words, my seeking connectedness verbally may be framed by my male friend as questioning his status and he may respond aggressively, defensively or dismissively. What I have said to him gets transformed into something other than what I intended.

Consider

- What difficulties might men have in seeking connectedness verbally?
- What difficulties might a woman listener have in recognising his verbal behaviour as seeking connectedness?
- How might this have an impact on a male counsellor/female client relationship?
- How might it affect a female counsellor/male client relationship?

Language, culture, class and counselling

I hope it is clear from this that language communication is extremely complicated and that social factors (such as gender differences) are an intrinsic part of the process. Many other factors also intervene. Culture is crucial because different cultures frame verbal communications very differently, and just as there is no gender-neutral language use, so there is no culturally neutral language use. Even within each culture where there are many different sub-cultures, there will be 'framing differences' which may cause misunderstandings and misinterpretations. I often feel that these are at least part of the basis of the 'Northerner/Southerner' stereotypes common in England, for instance, overlaid by the complicating factor of differing gender roles in one part of the country compared with the other. If this is so, how much greater might the complexities be when a person from one culture tries to communicate with someone whose cultural background is quite different.

Consider
As a group brainstorm some of the potential misunderstandings in communication which might arise in the following scenarios:
- a) an Asian counsellor with a white client,
- b) a white counsellor with an Asian client,
- c) a male black counsellor with an Asian woman client,
- d) a white female counsellor with a black male client.

• What conclusions does your group draw from this activity?

Language codes, class and counselling

So far I have briefly looked at the social aspects of language use as influenced by cultural and gender issues. I suggest that these differences are massively reinforced by class differences and, when class differences are part of the matrix of communication, the situation becomes so complex that I sometimes wonder how anyone ever understands anyone else!

Research suggests, as I have said, that different groups of people use language differently. I am not here referring to accent or pronunciation or even to vocabulary, but to the codes that exist within each language. A code is a particular way of using the language; for instance, I will use a different way of speaking (not just a different accent) depending on who it is I am speaking with.

Consider

Divide into groups of three, 'A', 'B' and 'C'.

    A speaks to B about their day.

    B plays the role of person A's close friend.

    A now repeats the exercise, but this time B plays the role of A's boss.

    C observes these interactions and makes a note of whatever differences in language use and ways of communicating   become apparent.

Compare your observations with other triads in your group.

• Were there common observations?

In some cultures the language rules formalise how we need to change codes for different audiences. In French, for instance, the word for 'you' is dependent on circumstances: 'tu' indicates intimacy and closeness while 'vous' indicates authority differences or lack of intimacy between the speakers.

In English, however, there are no *formal* words to indicate the degree of familiarity between speakers, yet there are many differences between the codes we use with different listeners. Some of these are necessitated by the content of what we are saying. It would be difficult to imagine Einstein discussing his theory of relativity with someone in a familiar relaxed code. Equally a company accountant is unlikely to give a verbal report to their Board of Directors in an informal and familiar code. In each of these examples it is the content of the communication which influences the selection of the code (though gender and cultural factors will also be influential).

It is not only the use of particular words which distinguish one language code from another, though this may be part of it. Neither is it accent, vocabulary or any other characteristic of the spoken word itself: it is the way in which the words and sentences are ordered and arranged – what is left out being a crucial part of this. In other words, codes have a structure which makes them different from one another.

Basil Bernstein (1971) claims that quite fundamental differences exist between the speech patterns of working- and middle-class people. He is not claiming that one is necessarily in any way better than the other (though I believe that socially one is more powerful and more valued than the other). Working-class speech patterns, he claims, are a kind of shorthand way of speaking – using what Bernstein calls a 'restricted code', meaning one in which a smaller vocabulary is used, there are fewer adjectives and adverbs and the syntax (how sentences are organised) is much more simple. Middle-class speech patterns on the other hand, according to Bernstein, are part of what he calls an 'elaborated code' that uses a more extensive vocabulary, more complex syntax and gives background information and explanations which are made explicit.

An example illustrating what he means would be that of a situation where some children are playing in a room when the phone rings. An adult in the room answers the phone but cannot hear because of the children's noise. Bernstein claims that, typically, if the adult is working class they are likely to turn to the children and say, 'Ssh,' or, 'Be quiet', whereas the middle-class adult might say, 'Be quiet for a minute. I'm speaking on the phone and I can't hear.' In other words the instruction in the second case contains background information and an explanation that makes sense of the instruction. The second message is much more complex than the first, the children are given a reason for the instruction, asked to empathise with the adult and are given a time frame within which they are being asked to be quiet.

For our purposes, in relation to counselling, the central point is that in the one case (that of a restricted code) the speaker is making assumptions about the listener. The speaker is assuming a shared context with the listener which makes sense of the content. In a counselling session, the counsellor may not be at all sure of the shared contexts assumed by a client speaking in a restricted code, and the client may well not know what the shared contexts assumed by a counsellor speaking in a restricted code are.

In the above example, the context for the children, however, is that they are playing and probably not very aware of or interested in the phone and who is speaking. For the adult, however, the context is different: they are trying to communicate in a noisy room. At this point they can make a decision to issue the instruction to the children without making the difference in context explicit, 'Be quiet', or issue the instruction by making the context explicit, 'I'm trying to speak on the phone and I need you to be quiet because I can't hear'. In the first case, the adult assumes the instruction will have meaning and will make sense to the children (in other words assumes they share the phone context with the adult). In the second case, the adult does not assume a shared context that makes the instruction meaningful, instead they make the context explicit so that it can become meaningful for the children.

One of the situations most adults have to deal with regularly is that of children coming home from a party or from school and giving a piece of information apropos of nothing at all. We cannot respond until we have more information about the context, enabling us to understand the significance of what the child is telling us. Once we have established the context, we can begin to understand the meaning and significance of the information. Young children, in other words, do not understand different contexts; they assume that the adult shares their context of meaning (which is sometimes the case, but often is not). As children get older and begin to understand this they will often begin a sentence with, 'You know so-and-so, well she ...' This is an attempt to provide a context of meaning that makes sense of what they are saying. It is not, of course, only children who do this.

Consider
• From your experience, what situations arise in counselling relationships that might give rise to the same assumptions about shared contexts?

Working in pairs 'A' and 'B':
>   A gives B some information about something that has happened to them recently involving people that B doesn't know. Do this without background information or explanations.
>   B listens and tries to grasp the meaning and significance of what A has told them.

• What further information did you need to make sense of what A was telling you?

• How did you get the information you needed?

• What did the information add to your understanding of A's account?

Bernstein claims that middle-class people have access to, and use, a restricted code as well as an elaborated code. The restricted code is used amongst close peers, friends and colleagues who share the context in question and within the family. They shift to the use of an elaborated code when the listener does not share the context that would make the conversation meaningful and even shift from one code to another within the same conversation where appropriate. In other words, the claim is, middle-class people adapt their speech code to the audience and to the context and content of what is being conveyed.

Working-class people, on the other hand, whilst they *understand* both language codes, tend generally to use a restricted code, assuming shared meanings even where this is not the case.

Most of these claims about language have been very influential in the field of education where they have been used to explain why many working-class children tend to under-achieve in terms of qualifications. The argument (a very controversial one) is made that use of a restricted code reflects and leads to less complex and less analytical thinking which in turn may impede the child's progress. Further, the claim is made that the extent of working-class children's capacity to grasp and express ideas may be underestimated by teachers when they are conveyed in restricted code. Whilst these claims (about the relationship between thinking and language) can be and have been challenged, there is no challenge to the claim that there are different codes and that they are differently 'powered' by their association with different classes. In other words, whether or not the use of a restricted code limits thinking is not what I am concerned with here; rather the issue here is the power relationship between the two codes. Because elaborated code is associated with the more powerful middle class it takes on a greater social value than the restricted code and thereby disempowers those who use the latter.

Consider

In your work or your training group, or in your network of friends:

- Can you identify those people who speak predominantly in one code or another?
- Is it possible for you to identify what impact that has?
    - Does it, for instance, mean that they are listened to more carefully?
    - Is the content of what they say listened to more attentively?
    - Are they perceived to be speaking with greater, or lesser, authority?

Language and counselling

If speech patterns are imbued with different amounts of power, as I believe they are, then it must be the case that those power relations enter into counselling relationships. As counsellors, in other words (whether our origins are middle or working class), we do not 'listen with a neutral ear', we listen to clients whose speech patterns have a direct effect on the power relationships. It may be, for instance, that a client who tells us their story in an elaborated code is taken more seriously, given more authority and thereby reduces some of the power imbalance between counsellor and client.

The reverse is also true. If we are told the story by a client in restricted code with the relative lack of power and authority this carries, we may underestimate the client's insights, sophistication and ability to make sense of their own lives and, unwittingly, we may reinforce the power imbalance between us.

Either way, the speech code is not neutral in its effect on how we, as counsellors, hear our clients. Neither does the client hear us neutrally, but with all the social power imbalances attached to our speech codes as counsellors, again contributing to the power differences.

Since counselling relies so heavily on speech, it seems to be of great importance that we remain continually aware of its possible implications.

Class codes and meaning

A further (and possibly even more important) way in which class and speech codes impact on counselling is by the assumptions we make about meaning structures.

Language not only describes the world as we perceive it, it actually constructs that world and is constructed by it. In other words, language is reflexive in that it both *describes* the sense we make of our world and *creates* sense of the world. An example of this is the concern with 'road rage'. It is likely that the kind of behaviour we now describe as 'road rage' has always existed, although we may not have previously described it as such. Once we create a term for that behaviour, the behaviour itself acquires a new meaning and significance. The process of creating a new phrase or word is not a neutral action – a word to describe a piece of behaviour indicates that it is significant (either positively or negatively), it has importance, and it is then given even greater importance once it is denoted by a word or phase. Language, in this way, is reflexive.

The language (and the language code) a client uses to enable the counsellor to gain entry into their internal frame of reference reflects the meaning of that internal world to the client. It is a kind of model that the client uses to represent the internal flux of their experiences. Yet we know from above that, as counsellors, we do not 'hear' this speech code neutrally and, even more importantly, if the client is using a restricted code, they are assuming a set of shared meanings with the counsellor. In this way, the internal framework that reflects the client's meaning will not be made explicit; background information, which might make the client's frame of reference accessible, may not be made available to the counsellor, and the client may believe that feelings, behaviour and events are self-evident and therefore they will not be verbalised.

If that happens (and it is much more likely to happen when the counsellor is middle class, is working with a working-class client and is unaware of the significance of that), then it is possible that:

a) the client may not feel 'heard' by the counsellor who may not feel able to ask questions which might elucidate the client's internal frame of reference, or

b) the counsellor may 'fill in the gaps' empathically from their own meaning structure, assuming it to be similar to that of the client, when in fact it may be a class-based meaning structure.

The client (because of power imbalances) may feel unable to challenge this even if it is made explicit (it might not be if the counsellor remains unaware of the possibility). To some extent it is possible to 'check out' with the client whether or not the counsellor is grasping the meaning structure, but a client who feels vulnerable and powerless may respond by agreeing with the counsellor, feeling this is what it 'should' mean. Either actively or by default the counsellor may impose their meaning system (which may be class-based) on the client and in this way inhibit, slow down and fail to facilitate the client's process.

I believe that this is a potential danger even with something as person-centred and basic to most counsellors as the offering of empathy as a facilitative skill. Empathy refers to identifying a feeling or set of feelings that I might feel if I were 'in the client's shoes', but what that feeling or set of feelings might be would be formed, at least in part, by who I am in terms of my gender, race and class. To the extent that I may be different in these respects from the client, it is likely that my feelings and responses may be quite different from those of the client. Again, I can check out the accuracy of my empathy, and in a power-neutral or equal relationship the client will feel free to respond without inhibition. However, this is not a relationship of equal power, particularly if class differences are involved, and the client might feel unable to contradict or correct the counsellor, or may even feel this is what their feelings 'should' be or 'should have been', giving too much weight and authority to what may be little more than a guess on the part of the counsellor.

The further away I am from a client in terms of social characteristics, the greater the likelihood that my empathic interventions may be class, gender or race-based and the greater the risk that the client may not be empowered to reject or dismiss them. The general assumptions with which we have all been conditioned (in this case 'the middle class knows best') are not left outside the door of the counselling room but come inside to contaminate understanding and increase the danger of the counsellor attributing meaning to client's experiences which are different from those of the client themselves.

Consider

To see whether these claims might apply to, for instance, congruence with a client, consider a counselling scenario where (a) they would not apply (b) where they would.

See if you can create a short scenario between counsellor and client where unconditional positive regard might be contaminated by any one of the claims made above.

Vocabulary and counselling

On a more basic level, I believe that social class impacts on counselling in the very words used by clients to describe their feelings. One of the main ways in which, as counsellors, we try to facilitate the client's process is by trying to highlight the feeling content of their experiences. We are trained to focus, not on the 'factual' components of what the client is telling us (and telling themselves), but to pay due attention to these factual components as a vehicle for expressing feelings.

Class has a direct effect, it seems to me, not on how the client feels (though it *is* probably a factor) but, more immediately, on whether and how the client expresses feelings. Many clients have a very limited vocabulary with which to represent sets of feelings which may nevertheless be experienced with great intensity. The limitations of the client's feeling vocabulary may (and I believe, with working-class clients, often does) misrepresent the intensity with which they may be experiencing their feelings and this may mislead the counsellor as to the significance of that feeling in the person's life. For example:

Counsellor: *I'm imagining that you must have felt sad when that happened.*
Client: *Yeah, well ... yes. I did feel a bit sad about it.*
Counsellor: *I think I'd have felt very sad if it'd happened to me.*
Client: *Well, like I said, I did feel pretty sad.*

The counsellor in this example is trying to facilitate the client getting in touch with her sadness and may well have done that, but the words used by the client give very little indication to the counsellor as to the depth or the intensity of the feeling experienced by the client. Further focusing might well be experienced by the client as pressure, and the counsellor might avoid any other invitations to elaborate in order to avoid this.

A particular response I often have difficulty with when working with a working-class client is a description of feelings so general that I can't get a sense of their importance because the client is using words which could apply to a whole range of emotions. When this happens, I not only don't know how important the feeling might be,

I am often not even sure what the specific feeling is. For example:

Counsellor: *What do you feel like when that happens?*

Client: *Well, you know, I feel bad about it and I don't like it but I don't know what I can do about it.*

Counsellor: *It sounds like you feel a bit helpless when that happens. Is that right?*

Client: *Well, yes, I feel bad and yes I know I can't do anything about it.*

Counsellor: *What does it feel like when you feel bad, do you feel angry or sad or what?*

Client: *Yes, like I said I feel really bad.*

I believe that this is an example of a situation where the counsellor's attempts to facilitate the client's expression of emotions are limited by the vocabulary of feelings available to the client. I believe, too, that in this situation the counsellor may well (without intending to) attribute a set of feelings to the client which may not reflect what the client is experiencing, and this may remain unchallenged by the client. I don't believe that it is a failure on the part of the counsellor to listen carefully, but rather that there isn't enough 'feeling' information being conveyed by the client to enable the counsellor to gain entry to the internal frame of reference. The temptation here is to become an interrogator and this is obviously not appropriate! It is a bit like being given a small torch with which to try to illuminate a large, dark room. We may be able to make out the general shape but the detail is still not visible.

Some clients in this situation may become very frustrated and irritated by 'silly questions', or they may feel they are failing as clients in some way that is not clear to them. Asking a client to convey to us the subtle nuances of their feelings may be experienced by them as an impossible task for which they do not have the verbal tools.

There are class differences (as well as gender and other differences) in the extent to which people can explore their feelings generally, and when these are brought into the counselling situation with its other inequalities of power, the potential for failing to empower the client is greatly increased.

Consider

Role play a counselling scenario with a partner, with a third person as observer.

The 'client' tells the 'counsellor', 'When my mother says things like that to me I feel awful.'

The counsellor's task is to elicit more information from the client about 'feeling awful'.

The client's task is to respond to the counsellor's probing by using no more than one (or, at the most, two) other feeling words.

- What did each of you feel during this role play?
- What did the observer notice about both the counsellor and the client?

I have made a number of claims in this chapter about the implications of language use in counselling, so it may be useful to give a brief summary here of the main points. I have claimed that:

1. All of our social characteristics (gender, race, class etc.) have an impact on how we communicate verbally, and how we respond to others' verbal communications.
2. A major factor in this is the amount of power attributed to us by the social group we represent to our audience and vice versa.
3. Language is not a single unitary system of words connected by syntax, there are different language codes within the language.
4. Each of these codes is differently 'powered' by the social group with which it is associated.
5. This has implications for the counselling process, and may disempower working-class clients.
6. Working-class clients may have a limited feeling vocabulary and this may result in their not feeling heard, and/or having their feelings misunderstood or misrepresented to them by the counsellor.

Chapter 4

Poverty, Class and Counselling

Overview
This chapter deals with poverty, the causes of poverty, the impact poverty has on people's lives, the ideas we have about poverty and how they impact on counselling.

I also look at the kinds of counselling available to people who are poor and examine the political implications of that.

Although language use is such an important aspect of class, affecting what goes on in a counselling situation, it is by no means the only important influence. Everything that symbolises class can be, and is, processed by us when we meet somebody. We categorise people we meet in a whole range of ways, some of them of importance only to us as individuals, such as whether we find them easy or difficult to make conversation with, whether we think they have a good sense of humour, or whatever else might matter to us individually.

As well as these personal preferences for particular qualities in other people, we also perceive and make assumptions about people on the basis of their gender, race or ethnicity, whether they are homosexual or heterosexual, disabled or non-disabled. These refer not to individual characteristics but to *social categorisations* and they have a great impact on how we relate to people.

Consider
In pairs list the qualities in another person that you look for when you first meet them. Share your list with your partner and see whether there is any overlap between your lists.

- Which characteristics are personal and which relate to some social category?
- What connections might these have to counselling?

It has been shown in most recent books on counselling that social characteristics have a direct impact the counselling process. The gender or ethnicity or any other social grouping may influence counselling (*see* Chaplin, 1990; d'Ardenne and Mahtani, 1989).

I agree with these writers that this is so, but I also believe that they leave out of their accounts how social class is interrelated with race, gender etc. When omitting class, I believe that they often miss something really important, namely that race, gender, and other social groupings vary greatly in their significance, and they vary on the basis of the class position which the individual occupies. I suggest that the experience of being middle class and black is fundamentally different from the experience of being working class and black, and that middle-class women experience the world quite differently from working-class women.

Consider
In a group:
- What differences are likely to exist between the experience of being a doctor who is black and an unemployed black person?
- Why might these differences matter in a counselling context?

While recognising the crucial importance of social issues in counselling, the discussions of these issues overlook what for me is a central fact: that class is far more important an influence on counselling than any other social grouping, and that each of the other groupings is mediated by class. By this I mean that I, as a white middle-class woman, am likely to have more common experiences with a black middle-class woman than either of us has with either a white or black working-class woman. Equally, a black working-class man has more shared experiences of living in the world with a white working-class man than either has with a white or black middle-class man. This is, I suggest, because class position is by far the greatest determinant of our life chances and experiences: greater than gender or race or disability or age or any other social groupings. It is greater because it mediates all other social groupings, reinforcing or reducing their impact on people's lives.

We can see some recognition of this in a number of fields. In America, for instance, the race riots in large cities resulted in government policies such as positive action in schools and universities, designed to enable some black people to overcome some of the obstacles to their progress by reserving places for them on degree courses. Employers are required to employ and facilitate the progress of black workers. This was, in effect, a deliberate policy attempt to create a black middle class who would have an economic stake in supporting the system in America. Such a policy recognises that class loyalty, class belongingness, is more important as a reference point and determinant of experience than race or other social groupings. As a policy it has indeed been very effective in promoting commitment to the system, despite some continued race riots such as those in Los Angeles. It is interesting, though not surprising, to observe that race riots have occurred in mainly working-class areas and have not, generally, engaged the support of middle-class black communities.

In Britain a much more limited attempt has been made to promote the emergence of a black middle class. Some attempts have been made to do this by funding a small number of courses originally designed to enable black people to re-enter education in order to train as social workers or teachers. It is worth noting, perhaps, that these course developed mainly in London, Manchester and Liverpool; all cities which have experienced race riots. This seems to me to suggest a recognition at some level (though not explicit) that black people's effective exclusion from the middle class can cause disenchantment with the system and so encourage black people to seek solidarity and support within their own communities to compensate.

The point of these examples is to illustrate my claim that class is of much greater significance than any other social grouping in affecting people's lives and that if we, as counsellors, fail to recognise and remain aware of this, we may make assumptions that all black people or all women, or whatever, are equally empowered. I am claiming that while race, gender etc. are major means of positioning people in a power hierarchy, they are not the most important means. Class is, I believe, far more important.

Consider
- As a counsellor, what sorts of assumptions might you make when an Asian woman doctor comes to seek counselling?
  - Would they be the same sorts of assumptions you would make if the Asian woman was a factory worker?
- What might be the dangers of giving priority to the woman's cultural experiences over her class experiences?
- What might be the dangers of believing that neither the woman's class nor her cultural background had any relevance for you as her counsellor?

One of the features of class that receives very little attention in counselling literature is economic factors. Little attention is paid to the way in which poverty, for example might have or have had an effect on a client's experiences of the world. Yet we know from our personal experience how important financial factors are in our lives and our experiences of childhood.

Consider
Working as a whole group:
- What are the main ways in which people's lives may be affected by poverty?

Working on your own:
- Were there any ways in which your life as a child was influenced by the financial status of your family?

Share this information with a partner and see whether there are any similarities.

Discuss with a partner:
- How might a client's experience of poverty or affluence impact their attitudes and experiences?
- Would it matter if the counsellor's experiences were very different? If so, why?

What we know about poverty suggests that class and poverty are very closely related. This is not to suggest that middle-class people never experience poverty, nor that all working-class people do so; it is to suggest that the vast majority of people who experience poverty are working class. We know, of course, that there are degrees of poverty; in other words that poverty is a relative concept and that the same income may be experienced by some people as poverty and others as sufficient for their needs. There is, in other words, a subjective dimension to poverty.

There is also, however, a generally accepted level of income per household below which a family or an individual is formally deemed to be living in poverty. In Britain (2003–2005), for instance, twenty eight per cent of children are being brought up in households which are formally designated by government criteria to be living in poverty. Almost all of these children live in working-class families.

We know that poverty affects people's health (through poor nutrition and poor housing), their life expectancy, their educational achievements, their aspirations, standards of dress, leisure activities, level of stimulation, and attitudes to themselves and other people.

Poverty is closely connected with self-esteem, we know (some of us through personal experiences) how difficult it is to feel good about ourselves when we feel poor.

Consider
- What sorts of feelings would you expect from a client who is very poor?
- What assumptions would you make about a very poor client?
- What assumptions might a very poor client make about a counsellor?
  - Why might these feelings and assumptions matter?
- How might poverty prevent a client from fully benefiting from counselling?

I believe our society teaches all of us to have very unsympathetic attitudes to poverty and, by implication, to people who are poor. Poverty carries with it a great deal of social stigma: it is something we are taught to be ashamed of. Most of us who work as counsellors would probably reject the idea that the poor are responsible for their own poverty. However, I feel that because it is not discussed in counselling literature it is unlikely that we will have escaped some of the commonest assumptions which are contained in the social ideology of opportunity to succeed.

Consider

As a group:
- Brainstorm and see if you can you produce a set of explanations for poverty which might be social and have little to do with how individuals manage their money.

Working on your own:
- What are your personal views and feelings about poverty?
- What have you learned by looking at poverty from these two perspectives?

Research suggests that the major causes of poverty, are fourfold:

1. old age
2. unemployment
3. low pay
4. inability to work through illness

The first of these is, of course, to do with government policies on the level of pensions to be paid to older people. Since it is less likely that working-class people will have had surplus income during their working lives to provide for their future, poverty in old age is very much related to political decisions connected with class.

Equally, unemployment affects working-class people disproportionately. In other words, class and unemployment are very closely connected. Levels of pay not only affect present income, they determine the amount of money people can use to provide for their future, and therefore low levels of pay produce poverty for the whole duration of the life cycle.

Illness as a *cause* of poverty is itself class related. We know that health and class are closely connected and that certain jobs badly damage health.

Poverty affects the poor in terms of whether counselling is accessible to them or not and where it is (for instance, with GP fund-holding practices), the client has no choice of counsellor, no control over the duration of the counselling and no control over the choice or type of counselling available. Obviously it is better to have some counselling than not, but the limitations of what is available to poor clients is another example of the way in which class differences impact on counselling issues.

Counselling in GP practices (and there are relatively few exceptions to this) tends to be 'problem-centred', and relatively short term and has to be seen to be cost-effective. None of these considerations is within the control of the client who would otherwise probably have no access to counselling except than through a voluntary agency. This is not in any way to criticise the work done by GP practice-based counsellors; it is to draw attention to the fact that counselling itself gets drawn into the 'unequal distribution of scarce resources' and that when we work in this setting we may be required as part of our contract to limit the sessions available to a client on the basis of considerations which have nothing to do with the needs of the client.

Choices, Class and Counselling

Class is visible: it is apparent in our dress, our table manners; our accents, our houses, our taste in cars, and where we go for our holidays, how we spend our leisure time, whether we read books and what kind of books we read, how much television we watch and which programmes we choose, how much we drink and what we drink, whether we go to church, how many children we have, what schools our children go to, whether we have formal qualifications etc. etc. – the list is almost endless.

So much are these pieces of information taken for granted that they are part of the air we breathe. They are not, however, just differences between us; they are differences that are part of a class category which gives us authority, status, power and choice, or one which limits our access to these and erects barriers to our seeking a greater share of them.

Counselling as an activity is usually about one individual (a counsellor) in a particular kind of relationship with another individual (a client) in order to empower and strengthen the client to gain greater control over their life by making choices.

I have suggested that a number of social factors contaminate this process and may impede it. The factor in question here is choice itself. I want to examine the link between class position and the choices available to clients. To do that I want to explore the term as it is used by economists. They make a distinction between 'choice' and ' effective choice', meaning by the latter, a choice that we actually have the power to implement. I might choose, for example, to be the Prime Minister but it is unlikely that it is an effective choice in that I do not have the power to implement that choice. This is, I believe, relevant for counselling.

If one of its goals is to enable the client to make informed choices, then it seems to me that part of that process is for the counsellor and the client to recognise the choices they might make which are unlikely to be effective choices – and why. If we do not operate with the awareness that there are social as well as personal obstacles which limit the effective choices clients can make – and enable the client to recognise which are social and which are personal obstacles – we are in danger of becoming one of those obstacles ourselves.

I believe that class position is a major factor in determining the range of effective choices a person can make, and that the range is much more narrow for working-class people than it is for others. There is nothing absolute or inevitable about this in the nature of things, but in our present political system it is the case that there are constraints placed on the effective choices working-class people can make. I believe that so long as class issues are seen to be something external and irrelevant in a client's counselling, we will not facilitate the client's awareness of the social constraints that exist and the possible personal costs of trying to overcome these.

Consider
Imagine the following scenario:

You are a college tutor whose role it is to give educational guidance to an adult who wants to come back to college to do a degree. The student is 28 years old, a lone parent, working class with no formal qualifications. She tells you that she wants to do medicine. You want to support her and encourage her to enhance her life.

• How would you respond?

[This situation, in its basic elements, represents what sometimes happens in counselling, with the added dimensions that counselling is not about giving advice, and our role as counsellors is to try to enter into the client's terms of reference.]

At present, given that we are not in our training or in our professional development encouraged to 'take on' class issues or to see them as having importance inside the counselling relationship, we can avoid this dilemma, and I do experience it as dilemma. But, once we acknowledge the importance of class issues, we have to address a whole set of choices and decisions which up to now we have been able to avoid. Some of these dilemmas appear in the box below.

Consider
- How do we 'take on' class issues?
  - Can they be accommodated while still remaining within the client's terms of reference?
- If we do not address the class constraints of the client's life, do we end up colluding with the unequal distribution of life chances?
  - Do we exceed our roles as counsellors if we do address class constraints?
  - Are we selling clients short if we do not?
- Does it reinforce power differentials between counsellors and clients if we do acknowledge class constraints?
  - Does it reinforce power differentials between counsellors and clients if we do not?

It seems to me that it is easier to acknowledge some of the other class issues mentioned at the beginning of this section, such as differences in manners, accent, houses and so on. I think that these are very important aspects of class difference, but it is easier to acknowledge that the client may be affected precisely because they are visible. A working-class client coming into the home of a middle-class counsellor may well be intimidated by the house or its contents but they are present, tangible and, most importantly, they are in the awareness of the client. They are, therefore, much easier to discuss and make part of what goes on in a session.

Consider
- Is there such a thing as a class-neutral counselling setting?
- What are the major differences in the dilemmas a counsellor faces when dealing with :
  1. the visible differences between classes, or the
  2. awareness of the class structure itself?

Chapter 5

Political Socialisation and Counselling

Overview
This chapter deals with the more overtly political context of counselling. In it I examine some of the political concepts which exist in this society and how we are affected by these. I then go on to look at the present political climate and the impact that has on counsellors and clients.

In the previous chapter I made the claim that, whilst counselling is about one individual in a particular kind of relationship with another, the social context of that relationship cannot be ignored. I have argued that we bring to the counselling relationship everything society defines us to be, together with social evaluations of each of our social characteristics. The counsellor brings to the relationship whatever 'amount' of power they are endowed with by society and, inevitably the client does the same thing. Social characteristics cannot be shed by an act of will as we go into the counselling relationship. We bring these with us just as surely and effectively as we bring our personal characteristics. What the client perceives is the sum total of our social and personal characteristics and whilst I am not claiming that they cannot, in principle, be separated, I *am* claiming that they are unlikely to be so if we deny their importance.

In this chapter I want to examine another set of influences which I believe has an impact on the counselling process: that is the specifically political ethos of our time and place. How counsellors are trained, regulated and organised; what political priorities predominate in our culture at any given time and what status, role and function the current political climate imposes on counsellors as a social group, are what I am concerned with.

One of the things that consistently struck me in my own training and, since then, in interactions with both counselling colleagues and peers, is their (undoubtedly genuine) perceptions of clients, and people generally, which are positive and respectful. I found (and still do find) it deeply puzzling when those same people do not put these views into some systematic political model of the world. It puzzles me because I see the views of my colleagues as directly deriving from a political model, yet political models are almost never discussed or referred to.

Looking at British Association for Counselling and Psycho-therapy (BACP) journals and other papers, this same puzzlement comes over me as I read or listen to what are clearly political views framed in non-political ways. I experience some of my colleagues distrust of political ideologies and I feel concerned that they believe that if they *do* have a political view of the world it is something separate from their activities as counsellors or trainers or supervisors. I find this deeply disturbing, particularly because the perceived absence of a political model of the world is directly imported into training programmes. This means that new trainees absorb the notion that ideas about counselling and political ideas *are* separate.

I believe quite the opposite: I believe that every single individual trainee, counsellor and supervisor, like every other person in the world, *does* have a political model which they carry about in their heads and which shapes and directs (amongst other things) their practice as counsellors, trainers and supervisors. Furthermore, I believe that each of us *does* have a model that exerts this influence; even when we are not aware of holding one in our heads – and even when we know we *do* have a political theory but we believe we keep it separate from our counselling activities.

I recognise that different people hold their political models with different degrees of awareness, but I am claiming that there is no possibility of *not* having some internal representation of the world which can be made explicit (though it may be, and often is, a confused and contradictory model). In other words, I believe there is no politically neutral fence available for us to sit on, and that our attempts to do so have the consequence (intended or not) of supporting the existing political system. When we try to be politically neutral, not only do we end up by being 'conservative' (in the sense of not challenging the status quo) but, even more importantly, we do this 'out of awareness', by default, and in this way we fail to take personal responsibility for the consequences of our actions or non-actions.

Children and political education

I have not introduced the arguments above in order to be critical of, or judgemental about, those people who generally believe they are 'not political' or that their actions have no political consequences. Rather, I would claim that these *beliefs* are *themselves* the consequence of political decisions made (by all political parties) not to include political awareness-raising and political education as a legitimate part of every child's education. There is enormous suspicion about the motives of anyone who tries to educate their children about political matters: it is treated as a type of indoctrination which exploits the child. This conceals all kinds of patronising assumptions about the integrity of the person doing the teaching and their motives for doing so. It also contains a set of damaging assumptions about children's ability to make up their own minds politically, once they have all the appropriate information.

We are conditioned, I believe, to be mistrustful of all political education and to see it as an attempt to impose a partisan political model on otherwise politically neutral people. Nothing could be further from the truth. Children as well as adults are continually exposed to political ideas, such as the 'advantages of advertising', or the 'desirability of competition', with no acknowledgement that these are political ideas, and very controversial ones at that. Because these ideas are 'framed' in a way that conceals their political nature, they are seen as 'given', as normal and ordinary, and therefore never, in principle, up for discussion. It is this I believe to be cynically manipulative, and it is the non-neutrality of the consequences of defining ideas as politically neutral in their consequences that I would like to explore in the next section.

I feel a need here to reiterate the main point I am making, which is that *our views and ideas are political in their implications even when we think we are apolitical beings*. This is not an attempt to change anyone's political ideas, but to argue that we do have them – counsellors and clients alike – and that this matters.

Consider

Try the following questionnaire. Its purpose is not to change any ideas you might have but to demonstrate that you do have views and that those views have a political dimension and represent a particular political model of the world. See whether you agree or not with the following statements:

1. People should provide for themselves and not rely on the state to do so.
2. The move to fund-holding by GPs has enabled them to provide counselling for their clients, and this is beneficial to everybody.
3. League tables published by schools give you greater opportunities to make choices about your children's education.
4. Competition between providers of services results in better quality services for people in the NHS.
5. In the next election, which party is voted into power will greatly affect everyone's lives.
6. The move to have counselling regulated by requiring individual counsellors to seek BACP accreditation is necessary and therefore should be welcomed by all responsible counsellors.
7. People who have strong political beliefs are likely to impose these on their clients.
8. The Trade Unions in Britain have been too powerful and it is a good thing that they have been controlled by government legislation.
9. I don't believe that politics is a suitable topic to discuss with people whose views don't agree with mine.
10. I don't have extreme political views; I believe I look at political issues in terms of how they might affect me or my family.
11. I find politics confusing; I don't know who to believe so I don't bother with any of it myself.
12. I believe all politicians are out to 'feather their own nests' so I don't even bother to vote because they're all as bad as each other.
13. I think that people's freedom to live as they want to is all I need to know about politics.
14. I believe that the tax system in Britain is reasonably fair, though I don't much like having to pay tax.
15. I think that poor people should be supported by the community.
16. There isn't any benefit to anybody in sending people to prison, we need to find other ways of dealing with criminals.

The political context of counselling in the UK

I have claimed that we are all political beings with political ideologies of which we may or may not be aware, and that our political ideologies have consequences for us as counsellors and may directly impact on our clients. Of course, the same is true of clients: every client is a political animal with a political ideology which includes views about the possibilities available to them and, of course, this also has consequences for clients. If, for instance, a client holds a political ideology that assumes that social inequalities are inevitable and/or desirable, it follows that they will explore only certain possibilities for their lives and rule out others (maybe without even knowing that this is what they are doing).

As well as this dimension (that of the political ideology held by the individual counsellor and client about their own lives) there are other dimensions of political ideologies which will have an impact on them. Some of these ideas are contained in what is not named, in what is taken for granted about our society. These will be contained in concepts like freedom, democracy and social responsibility. We are taught, implicitly, to believe in certain ideas that are almost never examined. An example of this is the belief that people, for instance in Britain, are politically 'free' whilst those in other societies are not. I do not dispute that there are different degrees of freedom available in different societies and different types of freedom too. But I also contend that the differences may be more *apparent* than *real*. There are many people in Britain who are not economically free, and this imposes many other non-freedoms on them. People who are poor are excluded from many effective choices, as we saw earlier. In terms, for instance, of Maslow's hierarchy of needs (1970), not being able to meet basic physical needs may well exclude us from attempts to meet any other needs. In other words, there are many people in Britain who cannot free themselves from want at the most basic level and, whilst it is plausible, it is actually fallacious to say that they are 'free' in some other sense just because there are no legal or overtly political constraints on their seeking other freedoms. Yet we are consistently told by political leaders that we live in a 'free democracy' and therefore receive many privileges and should take on many responsibilities.

I have suggested that the extent of the freedom people enjoy may well be exaggerated, and I want to suggest that the degree of democracy that characterises our political system is also overstated. Terms like 'democracy' are not, it seems to me, neutral words which describe a political system. There are words which are 'hooray' words (such as democracy) and 'boo' words (such as communism).

Consider

Brainstorm in your group and see whether you can think of any other *boo* words and *hooray* words which are used as though they were merely descriptions. The example that comes to my mind is the word 'Granny' or 'Nana' – could a 'Granny' be other than a *hooray* word!

- Did the words you came up with have anything in common?

- Were there any examples where a word seen as a *boo* word by some in your group was perceived by others as a *hooray* word?

- Is the term 'counselling' a *boo* or a *hooray* word?

- Does the term 'psychotherapy' have a different feel to it?

Some of the terms I have referred to as 'boo' or 'hooray' words fall into one or the other category because they lay claim to be describing something which has strong emotional connotations for us. The word 'plate' has few such connotations in most cases, it simply describes a particular object which has a particular function. Other words are different, they do not merely denote something, they connote other things. Many political terms which are in common usage in our society (and this is true in other political systems as well) are not literal descriptions of anything that exists at all, they are 'valuing' words, they refer to desirable states of affairs, something most people would value. Democracy is one such term: its literal meaning (government by the people for the people) bears little relationship to British politics, or for that matter, the politics of any known society. It is, rather, an ideal, one which has never been achieved (in any society as far as I am aware). Nevertheless, all political parties use the term as though they, and only they, can ensure its 'continued' existence.

Consider
- What aspects of our society do you see to be democratic?

- What aspects of our society do you see to be undemocratic?

- Can you reach a conclusion on the basis of the above as to whether you live in a democracy or not?

- Does it matter whether or not you call this society democratic?
  - If so, why? If not, why not?

Most present-day political scientists regard democracy in its original form (as government by the people for the people) as an ideal which cannot be achieved because of the sheer scale and complexity of highly industrialised societies. Many of them claim that the political system which exists is instead a form of 'representative democracy', meaning that people's needs cannot be conveyed directly to government but are instead expressed by voting for someone who will become their representative and who will try to influence government policies to pursue their interests. Those of us who do not directly participate in government can join pressure or interest groups and try to have an impact in this way.

Other political observers see our political system quite differently. They doubt the existence of even *that* degree of democracy, arguing that:

- Since our representatives are quite unlike most of the people they are supposed to represent, ordinary people's interests are hardly expressed and attended to at all.

- We might be able to have our interests expressed by representatives if we had greater control over who our representatives are to be. This decision is made by selection panels of the main political parties and the only choice the population has is whether to vote for that particular individual or not.

- Even this limited version of democracy can be challenged because no political party in recent years has actually formed a government on the basis of having gained votes from a *majority* of the country's population.

The point being made here is that we live in a political system which is misrepresented to us as being a democratic one, and that the framework within which political debates take place is never discussed or acknowledged. As a consequence, most of us simply take it for granted that we live in a democratic society and do not, ourselves, question this claim. In this way our thinking about political ideas is 'skewed' by a set of political assumptions which are never made explicit and never, for the most part, examined. We internalise the political ideology of our culture, and the political discussions we do have amongst ourselves, or that we hear on television, are mainly party political discussions about which group of politicians should have our vote in the next election. The political framework within which those elections take place has no forum for debate, it (the political framework) is a taken-for-granted 'given' within which power can be transferred to one political party from another.

Consider

In your group:
- If you wanted to know whether your course is run along democratic lines, what pieces of information might you need?

- Do you know the political ideology of your trainers?
  - Is this an important piece of information?

- How might the political framework of your course influence the training you receive as a counsellor or supervisor?

- Do you, as a group, feel that you have the right to this kind of information?

- What are your reasons for feeling that you do, or do not, have this right?

The political climate and counselling

We have been discussing fairly abstract ideas in the earlier section: ideas about the impact of political frameworks on us as voters and trainees as well as counsellors and trainers. In this section, I want to look at this in a more concrete way. I want to examine the present political climate and the impact this has on us as counsellors as well as on our clients.

The present political ethos and climate has evolved over a long period of time and in this has been greatly influenced by many factors – the move to a global economy, mass unemployment, the decline in world markets, the impact of developing countries on Britain's industry, the move to service industries and away from heavy manufacturing industry, amongst others.

Capitalism (the system where goods are produced in order to be sold for a profit) is inherently unstable, subject to booms and slumps, capable of providing high standards of living and removing them just as quickly. Political parties have different ideas, to some extent, about how the population can benefit from the high standards of living whilst being protected from the worst of the depressions which capitalism is predisposed to.

Historically, the major differences between the political parties could be summarised by their approaches to:

- how to manage the economy,
- how to distribute the benefits of capitalism between the different groups in society, and
- what policies to pursue when the economy slumps.

In more recent years, however, some of these policy differences have declined with consequences which have had a direct impact on counselling in a variety of ways.

The legacy of Thatcherism

I would contend that the Thatcher years have had such a profound effect on the political ideology of present-day society that it is difficult to understand some of the changes taking place in the development and organisation of counselling if we do not take account of the impact on all political parties of Thatcherite ideas. I believe these ideas have had, and continue to have, a profound effect on counselling in a variety of ways, some of which I will examine below. Whilst I am referring here mainly to the political climate within which counselling now takes place, I want to add a reminder that these changes have to such a large extent become an internalised part of our thinking and belief system that individual counsellors will inevitably bring them into the counselling situation itself, as will clients.

One of the most telling political slogans of the Thatcher years was the claim that, 'There is no such thing as society, there are individuals and their families'. This claim, that society is no more than the sum total of all its individual members and, as such, has no impact on individuals, goes against most of the claims I have been making, as well as the claims other counsellors have made about, e.g. the impact of racism on us as counsellors and as clients, whatever our racial origins.

I want to argue that this claim has had an impact on all subsequent political ideas and that despite the ideology of counselling, and its claim to be person-centred, it has had a traceable impact on counselling itself.

Traditionally, one of the differences between the two main social classes was that they had different images of what society looked like. The image associated with the middle class has traditionally been one of individualism: a belief in the fundamental right of each individual to pursue their own best interests. Added to this was a belief that hard work is rewarded by progress, status and financial reward – a view writ large in the Thatcher dictum. However, traditionally in Britain, another facet of this individualistic ideology has been the belief that, as individuals, we also have a responsibility to others to support them during times of hardship or vulnerability. Thatcherism could be defined as an individualistic ethic of personal reward for personal effort, *without social obligations to others* or, at best, a very limited social obligation to others.

Traditional working-class views of the world have historically been very different. The individualism of the middle class was replaced by a collectivist ethic: a way of looking at the world which emphasises group membership and group loyalty and which recognises that the well-being of the individual is not determined just by hard work but by combining with others to gain an improvement in life chances for the whole group. The early trade unions were an example of this ethic made practical, they were a recognition of the relative powerlessness of the individual to protect and further their own interests.

The Conservative party has traditionally upheld the middle-class perceptions of the world and the Labour party those of working-class people.

> **Consider**
> - Which of the above views of the world are more evident (if either) in discussions of counselling?
> - Which aspects of counselling 'fit' with either of these images of the world?
> - Which view of the world do you feel most comfortable with, and why?

In recent years, however, the differences which were once evident between the parties have greatly diminished. The undermining of a collectivist approach to the world has been so eroded by the thinking and policies of the Thatcher years that the ethic of individualism has been taken to extreme lengths even in areas where there was an overlap between the two parties.

> **Consider**
> - Can you identify any areas in which earlier differences between the two parties' policies have been eroded?

Part of this rise of individualism is evident in the mistrust for the social support of vulnerable social groups such as the lone parent, the elderly, or unemployed, and the suggestion that a 'nanny state' was emerging because 'too many' people were dependent on state benefits. (This is in the context of a world economy which is creating mass unemployment, where support for the family has consistently been undermined, where elderly people have had services withdrawn which allowed them to be cared for by their families, and so on.) In other words, the ethic of social support being undermined by 'rugged individualism' results in blaming the victim for their own difficulties.

The effects of market forces

A second major change produced by the Thatcher years is the emphasis on market forces, the idea that supply and demand, if allowed to operate without interference from government, will result in a 'lean and healthy economy'. The application of the concept of market forces to areas of society where the ethos is one of services leads to a variety of anomalies.

An example of this is the idea that every service we provide must be audited and must be cost-effective. Services must also be shown to be 'quality-assured'. A number of bizarre anomalies follow from this, some of them with direct implications for counselling.

It is extremely difficult to demonstrate that a service is cost-effective and also of high quality and, in fact, they may on occasion be mutually exclusive, so quantitative measures (easy to calculate and compute) have for the most part been adopted by organisations. Targets, performance indicators and other measurable indices have come to be used to measure the number of clients/patients/students to be 'serviced' by a particular number of resources. In this way, subjective dimensions of the satisfaction of the client have been 'enumerated out of existence' and 'through-put' has become a major criterion of our effectiveness as service providers.

Consider
Divide your training group into *A* and *B*.

A. Imagine that you are an accountant and you want to check on the quality and cost effectiveness of counselling in a GP setting.
  • How might you do this?

B. Imagine that you are a counselling co-ordinator for a number of GP counselling settings. You want to monitor the service provided in a person-centred way.
  • How might you do this?

My suggestion here is that the concept of market forces and the enhancement of market forces to its position of overriding importance, paradoxically may result (in the 'service' sectors of the economy) in a *reduction* in the quality of services as experienced by the client. That this is so is undoubtedly the case within the NHS where the present government has conceded that unit cost-effectiveness as a priority may lead to tragic inadequacies in provision, as for example, in the increased demand for hospital beds during the winter.

This is not to suggest that we should not be accountable to anyone, as counsellors in organisations, for the cost of our services, but to claim that often the pursuit of a quality service is not reducible to a cost-effective service.

It is not, in my view, a coincidence that there has been a rapid development and expansion in counselling in this economic climate, and, to the extent that this facilitates greater awareness of and access to counselling for more people, this seems to me to be a good thing. However, my concerns are that:

- In opening up counselling in organisations, counsellors are being put under pressure by the other aspects of the economy that run parallel to the greater employment opportunities for counsellors (such as targeting, pressures to be cost-effective and so on).

- There is a danger that the present ethos of individualism denies the importance of social factors in people's lives such as classism, racism, etc. In other words, I have an anxiety that the general emphasis on individualism may prevent awareness of the other dimensions of people's lives.

- The increased employment of counsellors in organisational settings may have other effects on counselling staff, such as requiring them to offer training, keeping their costs as low as possible, and maybe restricting the freedom of staff to limit numbers, or make other internal decisions which may be cost-effective but not counselling-sensitive.

Consider
You are a trainer in an organisation and you are instructed to run a counselling course which will be 'income generating', i.e. will bring money into the organisation.
 • What concerns might you have?

You are a trainer in an organisation. You want to run a course for a particular target group but you know that this will not be cost-effective.
 • What can you do?

I am very aware that some of these difficulties may be avoided and/or dealt with by education of employers in the nature of counselling, but whilst I am also aware that some employers are indeed amenable to learning about counselling and doing their best to provide appropriate person-centred provision, I also believe that pressure on employers to pare down costs by reducing, for instance, absenteeism, may limit their capacity to give priority to person-centredness.

I know that for at least some GPs for example, the legitimacy of counselling provision may be in a reduction of the number of patient visits to the doctor, or a reduction in the drug bill. An item in a BACP journal draws attention to a summary of a piece of research which correlated counselling provision in GP settings with the bill for prescribed drugs: it indicated that no link existed between an increase in the scale and intensity of counselling provision and a reduction in the bill for psychotropic drugs. The writer concludes:

> For counsellors working in primary care, these findings are cause for at least mild alarm. Many GPs may read these articles and pick up only the headline news: Counselling does not prevent anxious and depressed patients from needing drugs. (*Counselling*, May 1996, 7 (2): 118–19)

The implication here is that the main justification for the employment of counsellors in a GP setting is the reduction of the cost of drugs for the GP. It is difficult to estimate what pressures that priority imposes on counsellors working in those settings but it is not hard to imagine that it could produce at least some. My limited experience of this kind of work (and it is limited) has been not that the GP directly exerts pressure, but that I *anticipated* that it would be exerted, and behaved accordingly, monitoring the number of sessions much more carefully than I would in my private practice, when the client is in control and the decision to limit counselling sessions is not made by me.

Primary Care Trusts providing counsellors are equally affected by the purchaser/provider ethos within which they now operate. Competition to provide services may indeed have some benefits but even where this is the case it is far outweighed by the drive to reduce costs, whether by offering counsellors conditions of work which are unacceptable, such as precarious levels of security and continuity of employment, or providing them with inadequate levels of support. Many counsellors employed on an hourly basis in a GP setting have no security of tenure; no sickness benefit, no paid holiday entitlement and, as such, they are subsidising the cost of counselling in GP surgeries.

This climate of emphasising competition and cost-effectiveness has an impact on counsellor training. Most (though not all) training is carried out in further or higher education. The political climate has had a direct and tangible effect on these institutions. The funding of courses in this way has emphasised greatly the 'value' to the institution of a trainee's continued participation on the course. Staff are given recruitment targets which they have to meet in order to avoid financial penalties being incurred. Courses are expected to be cost-effective in all cases, and where they are funded by course members, the provision is expected to generate income. 'Drop-out rates' are a major source of pressure for staff providing training, and, combined with the massively increased workload on trainers themselves, many non-counselling considerations may affect course provision.

Consider
- On the course you are undertaking, what do you observe to be the major pressures on your trainers?
  - How many (if any) of these have an economic dimension?

The outcome of the political changes we have been discussing so far is that despite a hugely increased emphasis on the quality of training provision, much of this provision is under-resourced and consequently relies on very high stress tolerance by staff and commitment to their work way beyond what they are paid for.

Consider
Person-centred counselling claims to be radical and liberating.
- Can these flourish in this climate?

Chapter 6

Rogerian Counselling and Politics

Throughout the previous chapters I have been arguing that counselling is not a politically-neutral process. I have tried to show that it is a process which is engaged in from a political perspective even when the counsellor is not aware that this is so, and that however much we might like it to be a politically neutral activity, it is in the nature of all human activities that they have political implications and political consequences.

I have claimed that, if this is the case, then as counsellors, supervisors and trainers we make choices: either active, conscious choices, or choices by default (by not actively making them). This happens every time we counsel a client, or act as supervisor, or train a group of people. We choose whether to become aware of our own political framework of ideas or to avoid doing this. We deliberately choose whether to act on our political beliefs and accept responsibility for doing that, or to avoid acting on our beliefs in the hope that we will not have to accept responsibility for whatever implications that might have for the client. The choice of being non-political or apolitical is simply not available to us as counsellors, however much we might want that to be so.

I have tried to show that political factors such as class enter into counselling through power imbalances between client and counsellor; in the language the client and the counsellor use; in the different class-influenced meaning structures through which we speak and hear; in the different vocabularies and codes we use; and in the different class-based experiences we may have.

I have further claimed that if counsellor and/or client remain unaware of class influences (where class differences exist between client and counsellor), any power imbalances in the relationship may be reinforced. Where this is so the outcome will conserve current political arrangements and ideology. Where this is not so (i.e. where these are challenged and worked with by being made explicit) the potential exists, I believe, for radical social as well as personal change to take place.

Consider

Take the following scenario: A young woman becomes pregnant and, for personal reasons, decides to have the pregnancy terminated. She contacts her local GP who, though sympathetic, tells her they have no funds left for payment of this. The young woman comes to you for counselling, confused and distraught.

- How might you as a counsellor respond, (a) 'apolitically' and (b) 'politically'.
  - How might the young woman experience each of those responses?
- What might the consequences be of (a) and (b)?

Or imagine the following: A client who is a parent arrives at a session very distressed. Her child has been refused a place at the school that the client really wanted her to attend and where the child already has several friends.

You happen to know that there is an appeals procedure which can be initiated in the case of such decisions, and your client is not aware of this. You also know that there are a number of political reasons for the allocation of some school places.

- What are the possible ways in which you might respond to the client?
- If you withhold the information you have, has the client been empowered?
- Is there any response to this client in this situation which would be 'neutral'?

I believe that in this particular situation if we withhold the information we have, we are reinforcing the client's sense of powerlessness in the face of the decision about her child, and we are also reinforcing the power differences that exist between us and our clients. I am aware that it would feel 'risky' for me to give that information and I would actively have to make a decision about whether or not I should do so, and that the criterion on which I would have to make the decision would have to be couched (for me) in terms of ethical considerations and the likely outcome for the client. I believe that as counsellors we have to be prepared to make those difficult decisions and to take responsibility for them. What the client then chooses to do (or not do) with the information is their own choice and responsibility.

It follows from what I have said that I believe that knowledge is power and, as such, I have an obligation to share it appropriately with the client. If I do not do this I am (deliberately or otherwise) condoning the making of decisions by those in authority that adversely affect people's lives or limit their choices. If I share my knowledge I am at least creating the possibility of the client challenging that. At another level, in sharing the information I am 'modelling' people's helplessness in the face of the power of others to make decisions about their lives.

The central point here is that neither of those options is neutral, either in intent (once I am aware of it) or in terms of consequences. One option is conservative whilst the other embraces and pursues change.

What about Rogerian theory?

In this section I will try to relate some of these issues and arguments back to Rogerian theory and I will do this by asking several questions and then trying to answer them in the light of my claims about the non-neutral status of counselling.

The questions I want to raise and try to answer are these:

1. Is it the case that Rogerian person-centred counselling is inherently conservative? Is it predisposed to an acceptance of the political status quo or does it have the potential to be radically challenging of political systems?

2. Is it the case that the emphasis on the individual and the individual's internal frame of reference necessarily leaves external influences unchallenged?

3. Does the emphasis on personal self-transformation focus so much on personal choices and personal responsibility that individuals are seen to exist in a social and political vacuum that has no relevance for those choices and changes, and does this result in 'blaming the victim'?

My own view is that Rogerian person-centred counselling *does* have the potential to radically transform external social and political structures, as well as individual people (see, for example, Rogers, 1977 and 1980/1995). I believe that this approach is *not* inherently conservative of existing political arrangements and their social inequalities, but that certain preconditions need to be met if the potential radicalism of the approach is to be realised.

I have claimed throughout that counselling (Rogerian or any other sort of counselling and therapy) is inherently political and I have tried to show that social factors, such as racism, sexism, classism and so on, cannot be ignored in the counselling process without particular political consequences. I have focused largely on the absence of class awareness in counselling culture, and the implications of that, in order to illustrate the political nature of counselling. The feminist critique of Rogerian counselling draws attention to this, as does the literature on transcultural counselling.

There are, of course, different perspectives within the feminist critique, some of which see the need to become aware of gender issues as a kind of necessary general reform of counselling. Other critics see Rogerian person-centred counselling as inherently conservative and as leading to damaging consequences, especially, for example, for particular categories of women. In other words, some critics see the framework itself as a conservative one whilst others see its application in practice as having conservative consequences.

Ruth Waterhouse (1993), for instance, claims that the Rogerian framework, and person-centredness generally, ignores the political and social constraints of people's lives and how they are oppressed by them. She (and others) claim that the person-centred approach focuses on the individual as agent of self-change and ignores social factors like racism and sexism which oppress people and limit the extent to which the individual has the power to change. If no account is taken of the institutionalisation of oppression, the individual will be limited in their attempt to self-transform. Ruth Waterhouse claims:

> ... women coming into counselling can be particularly harmed as a result of the person-centred emphasis on 'self-transformation' ...
> [It] gives unwarranted weight to the individual's power to effect change in their everyday lives irrespective of material and socio-political constraints. (1993: 63)

Well, yes and no. I do believe that the claims being made here are valid. I believe that counselling which does not see women as positioned in a system of social and economic inequality may well do just what Ruth Waterhouse is claiming.

I believe this is the case in practice, when counsellors do not 'problematise' gender and they take male ideology as a given, and most of all when they ignore class issues. I do not, however, believe that this is a feature of the person-centred approach as such, nor do I believe this is inevitable, but rather that it happens only when we fail as individual counsellors to 'take on these issues'. The class issue, I have claimed, is of the greatest importance because all other social positioning is profoundly influenced by it.

In other words I do not believe that the person-centred focus on the individual *necessarily* excludes awareness of the social constraints of people's lives in principle, though I do believe it may, and often does, do so in practice.

It is, I suggest, perfectly possible to focus on 'the self-actualising tendency of the socially positioned individual'. Clumsy as this sounds it is, I believe, the focus of potentially transformative counselling; not merely the individual as they present themself in counselling, but the person as a socially positioned individual with a self-actualising tendency. If we hold on to this awareness, I believe it becomes much less likely that we will practise counselling in a way that disregards the oppressive external structures which form the restrictive scaffolding of people's lives. If we do not do this, if we lose sight of the external context of the client's life, if we ignore the gender, race, and particularly the class structures within which the individual is engaged upon the 'journey to change', then I do believe that person-centred counselling is indeed potentially limiting at best, and damaging at worst, to those clients who may be already oppressed by the external social constructs of their lives.

If we concentrate exclusively on the 'individual-as-presented' we are much more likely to see their present emotional difficulties as deriving from internal adaptations – but without reference to what necessitated those adaptations in the first place. Since adaptations are essentially ways of protecting ourselves, we need to be aware of what external threats the individual may be protecting themself against.

For example, a woman who has adapted by never seeking promotion in a firm known not to promote or support women beyond a certain level, might feel that her behaviour implied passivity or fear of success or fear of responsibility, when it is actually an adaptation to a threat of rejection external to herself, and a very real threat, not merely imaginary.

Consider

Imagine, for example a client who wants to train as a counsellor. They cannot afford to pay the fees to do the course and feel that if they had worked harder, or managed their income better the costs of the course would be less of a problem. They feel resentful, inadequate and 'not worthy' of doing the course.

- How might concentrating on just the individual's feelings reinforce the internal difficulties the person is experiencing?

- What are the responses available to you as their counsellor?

- What consequences do these responses have for the client's sense of self-worth?

If we do not examine the social factors which produced the client's poverty, and that result in counselling training being inaccessible to people who are poor, then I believe we are, in effect, allowing the victim to blame themselves rather than take responsibility for their circumstances and possibly feel empowered enough to challenge those circumstances.

There is a profound difference between the possibilities offered by Rogerian person-centredness when it is gender, culture or class-bound and those available to the client (and the counsellor) when it reclaims the radical potential I believe to be at the heart of Rogers' own approach.

The radical, liberating perspective offered by Rogers himself helps the client to become proactive by enabling them to recognise the possibility that their present behaviour may be a reaction to external systems of patterned oppression.

The 'safer' (or apparently safer!) option is much less risky for the counsellor. It offers something much more limited to the client whilst making far fewer ethical, political and personal demands on the counsellor.

It is this 'safer' option which I perceive to have become the norm in the present culture of counselling. This is evident from the belief that we are non-political, that the practice of counselling needs only adjustments like integrating the feminist or transcultural critique of person-centredness into our practice to ensure neutrality and prevent damage being done to clients. It may be that this shift from radical Rogerian person-centredness to a more 'watered down' interpretation of the framework is to some extent inevitable as counselling training becomes increasingly subject to bureaucracy within institutions which may not be conducive to the more radical interpretation I want to reclaim. Issues of accreditation, of validation of training courses, as well as other financial and administrative concerns, may well work towards the routinisation of training and the loss of what I feel is an invaluable dimension of Rogerian person-centredness.

Without wanting to appear flippant, it could also be said that there are difficulties anyway in embedding radicalness in theories when they have been propounded by charismatic figures such as Rogers himself. Historically, it is commonplace for theories to lose their 'sharp edges' when the person who proposes them is no longer around. Some might suggest that this can also be said of Christian ideas, for example.

I am saying here that, as I see it, Rogerian person-centredness is based on a theory of personality and personal development which has very radical implications both for society and for individuals (Rogers 1951, 1980/1995). Rogers himself saw the individual as a sociopolitical being who pursues both autonomy and connectedness; who needs independence but also needs to be in a supportive external environment; who can achieve an internal locus of evaluation and still value their social nature and who, with support, can challenge the external oppressions which constrain them.

Rogers recognised that emotional difficulties develop when, as individuals, we get the balance between our social and our individual self wrong, when we give up on our individual self in order to gain the support we need from outside. He recognised that we internalise oppression from outside ourselves even when it no longer operates, for instance when we continue to apply conditions of worth to ourselves which are no longer relevant to our present circumstances.

In his quietly revolutionary way, Rogers acknowledges the need to identify the external oppressions which we have internalised and for him it is these that person-centredness takes on. Sexism, racism and classism are all external controls over people's behaviour and it is no less than 'taking these on' that we commit ourselves to if we, as counsellors, want to see ourselves as being part of the solution rather than the problem.

Our commitment to this is what makes us, I believe, person-centred; not a particular set of techniques but a willingness to carry on examining ourselves and our awareness of what it is that limits us and our clients in our pursuit of self-actualisation.

Consider
- Is it possible, in your opinion, for a counsellor to be person-centred and not to be engaged in any kind of self-development?

I have argued here that Rogerian person-centredness is a radical perspective which makes great demands on both clients and counsellors; I believe if we regularly fail to challenge our own and our clients' internalised ideologies we lose the radical dimensions of person-centredness and turn it into a much less powerful force for change than it should be. I have argued that the absence of a class dimension in our awareness does just that: it disempowers the potential of the approach in ways that I believe misrepresent what it originally offered.

In brief, I believe that person-centredness is certainly about being *with* the client, but it is just as importantly about being *for* the client.

In the introduction to the 1995 reprint of Rogers' *A Way of Being*, Irving Yalom wrote of Rogers' Honorary Lecture to the American Psychological Association:

> The audience sat back, relaxed in their chairs, awaiting the expected mellow retrospective of a revered septuagenarian. Instead Rogers rocked them with a series of challenges. He urged school psychologists not to content themselves merely with treating students damaged by an obsolete and irrelevant education system *but to change the system*. [My emphasis] (Yalom, 1995: viii)

Chapter 7

The Role of the Counsellor

Whose side are we on?

> **Overview**
> In this chapter I will look at how the role of the counsellor is
> a product of its time and how the way in which we define
> ourselves as counsellors, and what we 'should' and 'can'
> achieve, is constructed according to the wider political and
> social climate.

In the previous chapter I made the claim that Rogerian person-centred
counselling is based on a radical framework of ideas which I believe
has never reached its potential as a socially and personally liberating
approach.

I argue that part of the reason for this (and there are many,
some of them overtly political) is that the approach has, to quite a
considerable degree, been appropriated into mainstream culture
without the political dimension which makes it potentially radical,
and which I believe Rogers himself tried to develop. Just as the more
radical version of counselling proposed by Rogers was a product of
its time (including and particularly, the political climate of its time),
so the more depoliticised version of person-centredness seems to me
to be a product of recent political ideas, perceptions and values.

I have suggested that just as the cultural beliefs of present-day
society reinforce notions such as classlessness and the ideology of
the individual's right to pursue their economic and other freedoms
without reference to the well-being of others, so too was the radical
dimension of person-centredness a product of the cultural notion of
its time. As economic climates change from 'progress' and 'freedom'
to recession and economic stringency, and cyclically back again, so
too do cultural ideas – they change to fit the altering political and

economic circumstances. The roles of counselling and counsellors also change to reflect these different economic circumstances.

In other words, counselling does not take place in a social or ideological vacuum: it is a product of its time and place as much as any other cultural product and, if this is the case, it follows that counselling itself will reflect the political ideas of the present – that class, for instance, is no longer an important influence on people's lives – and other perceptions of just how things are.

An important characteristic of present-day culture (including political ideas) is the denial of the external influence of structures which create institutionalised racism, sexism and classism. These structures *do* have a 'reality' outside of each individual and do exercise constraints on individuals, but they do not exist independently of our reproducing and maintaining them. They are not fixed and immutable (however the individual might experience them); they exist and persist because human action recreates them. In this sense we cannot, either as individuals or as counsellors, avoid having an impact on structures; we are either oppositional in our relationship to them or we are accepting of them.

I believe that this charges us, as counsellors, with special responsibilities if we really are aiming for human fulfilment and liberation (and I believe many other groups of workers have similar responsibilities). Counsellors actively make claims to be in the business of human liberation and that differentiates us from many other 'people' workers, such as, for instance, social workers. One of the responsibilities this charges us with is to identify the 'unfreedoms' of people's lives, however much doing this is in conflict with others' definition of our role.

There are many pressures on us to define the role of counselling in narrow and limited ways; some, as I have argued are connected with the political climate, some are internal pressures and others come from the present culture of counselling itself.

Demands are made on us as counsellors to produce practical returns on investment in providing counselling services for employees. In industry there might be an expectation of a reduction in absenteeism or an increase in productivity, when we may feel that employees need time off and/or need to work less hard to reduce their level of stress. We may feel pressured in education establishments to have an impact on retention rates or examination results. We might feel that the institution measures our success in these terms (and that may indeed be so) when we as counsellors might want to empower students/employees to challenge the goals of the organisation or at least try to influence them.

We cannot assume that we can remain 'above' these commercial considerations (though we may try to be creative in ways of circumventing them). We are inevitably bound up with the organisation's system of values and accounting and this becomes increasingly an issue for us as we gain acceptance in different areas of the job market.

The same dilemma, I have argued, applies to the training of counsellors, where the pressure to increase and retain the number of trainees on courses can be extremely difficult to resist and where the result may be the exploitation of both trainees and their trainers. One of the casualties of this conflict of interests is often, I suspect, the person-centredness of the training and the loss of some of the more time-consuming and demanding features of training, such as making sure that trainees have an awareness of the political issues which will impact on their work with clients.

A further pressure (and, I believe, an increasing one) comes from the need to regulate counselling itself. This is such a complex and difficult area that it warrants a much more detailed analysis than I can give here in order to do it justice, although I will briefly introduce some of these issues in the next chapter. The need to protect clients and to protect and/or support counsellors has led to the increased professionalisation and bureaucratisation of counselling, and whilst few would disagree with the need to have some underpinning of standards of training and practice, there are also, in my view, many dangers in standardising and centralising, for instance, accreditation, beyond that of accrediting particular training courses.

I do not believe that the tendency to require individual professional counsellors to seek accreditation is just the result of a desire to protect clients (there is no research that I can find to suggest that accredited practitioners have a lower incidence of client abuse than non-accredited practitioners), nor do I believe it to be motivated by a desire to extend the client's choice of counsellor. However, I *do* believe that the tendency to ever-increasing levels of accreditation can be more easily understood in terms of political and social pressures on bodies associated with accreditation issues, such as BACP. They are being controlled by criteria which have little or nothing to do with the quality of counselling from a client's perspective.

Bureaucracies develop their own goals, which may have deviated considerably from their original aims. They may even begin to militate against the best interests of the client group they were designed to serve. There is nothing unusual about this, we can see evidence of it in many areas of social life; in the NHS where the welfare of the patient may become marginalised by the pursuit of bureaucratic goals; in education, where administrative requirements make it almost impossible for teachers to be child-centred.

All these tendencies point to ways in which counselling itself is influenced by factors external to the process of counselling, and it is very difficult to preserve some of the tenets of counselling in the face of these pressures. Many external factors have already been imported into counselling culture, depoliticising it and making it very 'risky' for individual counsellors to retain an emancipatory view of counselling, even within the profession itself.

I do believe that many counsellors perceive themselves to be separate from these external factors and I have tried to demonstrate this by drawing attention to the significance of the absence of class-awareness in counselling ideology, and to some of the consequences of that.

I have tried to persuade readers to the view that if we do not recognise the dangers of our attempts to be neutral, we are creating the possibility that we may become an agency for social control, enabling clients only to accept the unacceptable by defending (by default or deliberately) the indefensible.

Chapter 8

On Becoming Respectable
Regulation, professionalisation and accreditation

In the previous chapter I claimed that, as counsellors, we need to decide what our role is in relation to clients. I looked at how I perceive counselling to have lost its 'cutting edge' as a potentially radical force for social as well as personal change. I believe that nowhere is this more evident than in the recent moves to 'professionalise' counselling as a means of regulation and the increasing pressure on counsellors to seek individual accreditation through BACP.

There is nothing new about groups of workers using strategies to separate themselves and their skills from other groups of workers. Historically, many white-collar or non-manual workers have done this ever since a labour market has existed. One particular group who have been remarkably successful in becoming a separate segment in the labour force are those 'professionals' who were formerly perceived as 'workers'.

Consider
- How would you define a 'professional' as distinct from any other worker?

Work in threes to develop your definition, then compare it with others in your group.

- Were they similar? If so, in what respect?
- How did your definitions differ from each other?

Try the following exercise after you've defined what a profession is.

- Which of the following occupations do you see as a profession?

Bricklayer	Residential care assistant
Window cleaner	Radiographer
Doctor	Personal assistant
Shop assistant	Road sweeper
Sales representative	Secretary
Dentist	Funeral director
Carpenter	Gardener
Chiropodist	Tailor
Social worker	Housekeeper
Security guard	Politician
Physiotherapist	Book-keeper
Baker	Soldier
Nurse	Accountant
Chef	Mechanic
Counsellor	Vicar

- What were the criteria you used to decide which was which?

- What advantages does the individual gain when their occupation is perceived as a profession?

- Within the list of occupations you categorised as professions which were (a) well established (b) newly established and (c) in the process of becoming a profession?

Many definitions exist in literature: Millerson (1964) for instance, identifies the main features of a profession, as follows:

- the skills used in the work are based on theoretical knowledge;
- there is a relatively long period of training for the job;
- there is a set of values connected with the work which emphasises public service and altruism;
- a code of ethics is adhered to by those who engage in the work;
- workers insist on the freedom to regulate themselves;
- a body exists which tests the competence of members before entry is permitted.

Many groups of workers may fit this description in every respect, yet are not seen as professionals. For instance, house builders may now belong to a central organisation which is designed to protect house buyers, yet the building industry is not generally regarded as a profession. This is not to say that this will always be so, since occupations migrate from one status to another over time, so that at any one time we can distinguish between established, marginal and new professions.

To varying degrees, professions have been better able than non-professions to claim high status, greater autonomy and more money. Generally speaking, the more established an area of work is as a profession, the more highly paid and prestigious are its members. For instance, in a GP practice the doctor is a member of an old established profession, the practice belongs to a newly established profession (comparatively) and the reception and administrative staff are seen as non-professional 'support workers'. This will be directly reflected in their incomes and their status (as well, probably, as the number of days holiday they have each year). It is clearly a great advantage to belong to a profession in that it confers a number of privileges on its members. This can be interpreted in different ways.

One interpretation would be that the role of the professional worker is unique in the sense that a special relationship exists between professional workers and their clients; that the work engaged in involves that which is valued by most people in society (such as health or justice or education) and that this work therefore deserves special status and recognition.

This interpretation suggests that, because of the special relationship between the professional and the client, professionals have to institutionalise various procedures and norms to protect clients. These might include:

- socialising prospective professionals during training into particular values and norms;
- having a formal code of ethics;
- disciplinary procedures to control the behaviour of workers, and
- having a qualifying process by which the competence of the professional in ensured.

Consider
Discuss BACP amongst your group and see whether it fits with this interpretation of professionalism.

- What would you conclude from this about counselling as an activity?

Certainly, BACP as an organisation does seem to have procedures which would qualify counselling as a profession. It recognises certain courses as being appropriate for the training of entrants to the job; it does have a code of ethics to regulate the standards of practitioners;

and it does emphasise the special relationship between counsellor and client and, most importantly, BACP claims to be about the protection of clients.

However, other interpretations are possible and I suggest more closely reflected are the functions of BACP which are rarely discussed – that the organisation may operate more to protect and advance the position of the counsellor than that of the client.

I am suggesting here that moves to professionalisation are more about gaining market advantage over other workers than about clients. This is not to suggest that this is the motive of individuals within the organisation, nor that BACP does not have valid roles in other respects (as a network of support for counsellors and a forum of discussion for counselling issues, amongst other things). It is to suggest that BACP is, in effect, an interest group within the economy, (very much as trade unions are), designed to enhance the market position of a particular group of workers. I have no objection to this: what I do object to is couching the interests of counsellors in terms of the interests of clients I see BACP working to the benefit of professional practitioners, not the public and not the individual client.

I would suggest that the projected image of concern for the protection of the client, public concern and altruism, and the ostensibly disinterested practice of counselling, constitutes an ideology which may be used to protect and justify higher prestige and to prevent encroachment by other workers in an area of work.

This, it seems to me, is a further move towards creating a monopoly of control over entrants who wish to work as counsellors and will, in effect, result in BACP becoming a monopoly 'qualifying association', as the British Medical Association (BMA) is for doctors, or the Institute of Chartered Accountants is for accountants. (For more information on BACP codes and regulatory schemes see p. 89.)

One outcome of this would be to give BACP control over the right of entry to counselling and thus over the number and types of practitioners. In economic terms, of course, this would control the supply of counsellors and, with increasing demand for counselling, practitioners would then be able to command higher rewards and greater prestige.

This is precisely how the BMA operates. It has monopoly control over entry, qualification, accreditation and the right to practise, to the extent that it is illegal for a doctor not to be on the medical register. Legal monopoly confers even greater privileges in that it ensures dominance within a whole area of work, creating a hierarchy of money, power and prestige within health care. Related professions like chiropody have come to be seen as 'supplementary to medicine' and are subordinated to the authority of doctors.

Debates in counselling, clinical psychology, psychotherapy, etc. all suggest that whilst, as yet, no legal monopoly has been established there is evidence of the emergence of a hierarchy in the 'helping professions'.

Consider

Brainstorm in your group and see what comes up around the term 'therapy'. Do the same with the term 'counselling'.

- What (if any) were the differences?
- Were any differences related to prestige or money?
  - If so, what does this suggest.

The move to ever-increasing levels of accreditation is based on the assumption that greater levels of accreditation offer greater protection to clients. As I have said earlier there is no evidence to justify this view (nor to discount it either). But the process of seeking personal accreditation is such that no sensible counsellor is going to present for accreditation evidence of their work which shows them in a poor light. Rather, the counsellor is likely to present 'safe', uncontroversial ways of working which will not rock the boat or cause raised eyebrows. It would be plain silly to do otherwise and, in the light of this, it is difficult to see how further accreditation would protect clients. Supervisors' reports over a period of time are much more likely to give a representative view of how a counsellor works, and even this is of limited use, since an unscrupulous counsellor can conceal aspects of their work from supervisors.

If increasing levels of accreditation offer clients little in the way of a guarantee of increased safety, they may, nevertheless, offer counsellors greater job opportunity and demarcate them from other counsellors or other practitioners in the field.

Consider

Imagine you are on an interview panel of an company about to appoint a counsellor.

- What kind of job description might you devise?
- How might you try to ensure that your workers will be safe from abuse or exploitation by the person you appoint?
  - What are the implications of this?

Increased levels of accreditation, it seems to me, are more likely to inhibit than to facilitate creative and imaginative ways of being with a client; they are likely to reduce counselling activities to their lowest common denominator and more likely to lead to mechanical strategies than to being 'transparently real' to the client. They are then 'safe', but for the counsellor not the client.

An example of how this pressure toward conservatism works through increasing regulation is the reaction of certain elements in the counselling world to the publication of Brian Thorne's (1987) *Beyond the Core Condidtions*. Rather than debate the theoretical or practical implications of such radical work, some sought to censor it through appealing to regulations and codes of practice, thereby preventing any debate, stifling creativity and supporting the status quo.

Personal integrity cannot be measured by observing competencies: these are necessary but not sufficient. There is no means whereby we can use accreditation procedures to eliminate potentially abusive or unscrupulous counsellors; integrity is a personal characteristic, the absence of which can easily be concealed and the presence of which cannot be measured. It is misleading to clients and to employers to imply otherwise, and I suggest that it is inappropriate to allow what is, in effect, an occupational strategy to appear to offer protection to the public. Ultimately, clients are protected by the integrity of their counsellors, not by a political jockeying for advantage between different practitioners or their organisations.

The ideology of regulation is being challenged from within counselling and therapy. Examples include Richard Mowbray's (1995) book *The Case Against Psychotherapy Registration* in which he draws attention to the occupational–political context of registration and regulation of therapy, and Brian Thorne (1995) in his article *The Accountable Therapist*.

> **Consider**
> - What options are open to a counsellor who does not feel it appropriate to apply for personal accreditation?
> - How might they be disadvantaged by deciding not to apply?
> - What implications might this have for clients?

There are difficulties, too, with seeing a code of ethics as being exclusively concerned with the well-being and safety of clients. Clearly, the vast majority of counsellors would agree that certain kinds of behaviour (such as having a sexual relationship with a client) are completely inappropriate, while most counsellors see the existence of a code of ethics as a statement of how they should behave in relation to clients. However, I suggest that, again, this is largely a matter of personal integrity, and the extent to which a client is able to gain redress from abuse after the event is only partially related to the existence of a code of ethics.

Professional codes often prohibit or inhibit one professional publicly criticising another and it is in the nature of abuse which takes place in private that it is difficult to present satisfactory evidence with which to discipline a practitioner. Where they do exist in occupational groups, complaints procedures and codes of practice are often perceived by the public to be untrustworthy. What faith do *you* have in the procedures available to you to complain about doctors, solicitors or the police? To what extent may your answer be influenced by whether you are middle or working class?

I am not suggesting here that we should not have a code of ethics, but that codes offer protection as much to the counsellor as to the client. Yet it is for the purpose of agreeing a code of ethics that the professionalisation of counselling is being pursued.

> **Consider**
> You are a client from an ethnic minority community. You feel that you are being treated by your counsellor in a way that is racist.
> - What do you do?

- What information do you need to have before you can take action?
- What skills do you need to have to do so?
- What emotional resources do you need?
- What course of action are you most likely to take?

I have argued that moves towards the professionalisation of counselling, whatever the motives, are more about advantaging counsellors over other workers than furthering the interests of clients. Professionalisation is actually a *political activity* disguised by being couched in terms of an ideology that highlights the advantages to clients. I have claimed that clients are protected by the personal integrity of the counsellor and by counsellors scrupulously bringing their work to supervision, *not* by establishing counselling as a profession – whatever benefits this might ensure for them.

The socialisation of counsellors

I said above that one feature of the professions is that entrants are exposed to a process of socialisation into the profession. By this I mean that entrants undergo a process of learning that is not overtly part of the stated learning outcomes in terms of skills or competencies. There is nothing necessarily sinister about this: almost all learning experiences contain elements of 'hidden learning' such as a set of values and/or attitudes. In the formal primary education of children, for example, there is an explicit curriculum (the skills and knowledge content that the child will be taught) and what is known as the 'hidden curriculum': the norms and ways of being that are valued in this culture. These may involve 'sharing nicely' or 'playing well together' or 'being kind' and they are a very important aspect of what a child learns at school.

At secondary school the hidden curriculum may be very different and may be about the importance of competition, of achieving, of being a certain kind of student. This hidden curriculum has an all-embracing influence on children at school.

> **Consider**
> • What did you learn from the hidden curriculum at your
>   school?

The hidden curriculum as it exists in education is about socialising the child into being prepared for a particular kind of role in society.

Adults are also socialised into their roles by hidden learning processes that emphasise 'ways of being' and are intended to become part of that person's identity. Doctors, for instance, not only have to learn a body of knowledge, they must also learn how to take on the identity of 'doctor', which in this society has connotations of being respectable, caring, responsible, etc. This process of socialisation is made evident by the fact that medical students are often perceived to have opposite characteristics and that there is a noticeable difference between the stereotype of the medical student and that of the doctor. Part of this socialisation process is to 'unlearn' the characteristics and ways of behaving associated with being a *medical student* before taking on the new role of *qualified doctor* with all its associations of respectability.

This is particularly important for professions in which the rewards of high pay, status and trust, are justified by the responsible attitudes of professionals towards their clients.

I believe this is relevant for the training of counsellors; that our training involves not just the acquisition of skills and competencies but the learning and taking on of a particular identity – that of the professional. In doing this, training is often experienced as demanding, stressful, and often frightening and demoralising.

Most people who enter counselling training already have many 'counselling skills' learned from other roles, yet I know, both from personal experience and discussion with others, that trainees can feel very de-skilled and incompetent.

The process of socialising trainees into the identity and role of counsellor is about much more than learning theories and acquiring competencies, it is also about perceiving counselling as being not only different in degree as an activity, but also different in kind. It is as though training *requires* trainees to feel unskilled and incompetent in order to mould them as counsellors into a particular kind of person; not just a person having particular kinds of knowledge and competencies. It seems to me that this process is about moulding people into a particular view of what it is to be a professional and, again, I would claim that this is more about the requirements of the profession than the requirements of the client.

Consider
- Since coming on your training course have you felt de-skilled?
  - If so, what effect has that had on you?
  - What effect does it have on your work with clients?
  - Who benefits from this de-skilling?

I suspect that the results of this process of socialisation are to the benefit of the profession in having relatively compliant workers, and that the consequence for clients is that of having counsellors who conform to the standard image of the profession. The cost of this is likely to be to clients in having counsellors who are wary and frightened of 'being themselves' – real people in real relationships with real people. Without doubt a situation largely at odds with the fundamental tenets of person-centredness, which is concerned with congruence, transparency and being real. Again, the challenge to person-centred counsellors and helpers of all persuasions is to answer the question, 'Whose interests are you serving?'.

Consider
- Which 'bits' of yourself do you bring to your work with clients?

- Which 'bits' do you not bring?

- On what basis do you select which 'bits' to bring.

- Who benefits from your selection?

Conclusion

Throughout these chapters I have been putting forward my view that political issues affect counselling at every level, from the impact that social class has on counselling to attitudes to poverty and the impact of present political ideology on how we operate in our practice.

I have tried to show that political ideas have implications for the training and accreditation of counsellors and on the particular interpretation of person-centredness which informs how we work.

In doing this, I have clarified some of my own ideas about how I perceive the activity of counselling and, whilst I am aware there may be many who find some of these unacceptable, I hope that this will lead to honest and open debate between colleagues, trainers and trainees.

I do not claim to have the solutions to any of the dilemmas that some of these ideas raise for us, but I feel that it is important that we formulate the problems, nevertheless. How *can* we cross the class divide between the counsellor and client, where it exists? How can we make counselling more easily accessible to people who are poor? How can we reconcile person-centredness with political ideology, or be above these influences? I don't know the answers to these challenges, but I do know that avoiding them, or pretending they do not exist, is not the solution.

How can we try to ensure that counsellors can earn a reasonable living without being elitist, and without being unduly influenced or pressured by accountancy criteria which limits the type of work we can do or the quality of work we engage in? Again, I do not know the answer, but I do know that being swept along by whatever political 'flavour of the month' happens to be approved of by those in power is *not* the answer.

How can we develop some consensual code of ethics which goes as far as it is possible to go in protecting clients whilst leaving individual counsellors free, safe and supported enough to pursue the goals espoused by Rogers?

If some of these issues are discussed and debated openly and constructively, then I will believe these chapters have served their purpose.

References and Further Reading

References

Bernstein, BB (1971) *Class, Codes and Control.* St Albans: Paladin.

Chaplin, J (1990) *Feminist Counselling in Action.* London: Sage.

D'Ardenne, P & Mahtani, A (1989) *Transcultural Counselling in Action.* London: Sage.

Lynn, J & Jay, A (1983) *Yes, Minister, Vol 3.* Sittingbourne: BBC Books.

Maslow, AH (1970) *Motivation and Personality* (2nd edn). New York: Harper & Row.

Millerson, G ((1964) *Qualifying Associations.* London: Routledge.

Mowbray, R (1995) *The Case against Psychotherapy Registration: A conservation issue for the human potential movement.* London: Transmarginal Press.

Rogers, CR (1951) *Client-Centered Therapy.* Boston: Houghton Mifflin.

Rogers, CR (1977) *On Personal Power.* London: Constable.

Rogers, CR (1980/1995) *A Way of Being.* Boston: Houghton Mifflin.

Tannen, B (1987) *That's Not What I Meant.* London: Virago.

Thorne, B (1987) Beyond the core conditions. In W Dryden (Ed) *Key Cases in Psychotherapy.* London: Croom Helm. Reprinted in W Dryden (Ed) (1991) *Person-Centred Counselling: Therapuetic and spiritual dimensions.* London: Whurr.

Thorne, B (1995) The accountable therapist. *Self & Society, 23*(4).

Waterhouse, R (1993) Wild women don't sing the blues: A feminist crtique of person-centred counselling and therapy. *Feminism & Psychology, 3*(1), 57–71.

Yalom, I (1995) Foreword. In CR Rogers *A Way of Being.* Boston: Houghton Mifflin.

Further Reading
Ideology

Berger, P & Luckman, T (1963) The Sociology of Religion and the Sociology of Knowledge. *Sociology & Social Research, 47,* 417–27.

Kuhn, T (1972) Scientific paradigms. In B Barnes (Ed) *Sociology of Science.* Harmondsworth: Penguin.

Luckman, T(1967) *The Invisible Religion.* London: Collier-MacMillan.

Mulkay, M (1979) *Science and the Sociology of Knowledge*. London: Allen & Unwin.

Sharp, S (1976) *Just Like a Girl*. London: Penguin.

Language

Bernstein, B (1971) *Class, Codes and Contact, Vol 1*. London: Routledge & Kegan Paul.

Bowles, S & Gintis, H (1976) *Schooling in Capitalist America*. London: Routledge & Kegan Paul.

Byrne, D et al. (1975) *The Poverty of Education*. London: Martin Robertson.

Hand, N (1976) What is English? In G Whitty & M Young, M (Eds) *Explorations in the Politics of School Knowledge*. Driffield: Nafferton Books.

Stubbs, M (1990) *Language, Schools and Classrooms*. London: Methuen.

Poverty

Coates, K & Selburn, R (1970) *Poverty, the Forgotten Englishman*. Harmondsworth: Penguin.

Field, F (1993) *An Agenda for Britain*. Harmondsworth: Penguin.

Mack, J & Lansley, S (1985) *Poor Britain*. London: Allen & Unwin.

Hutton, W (1995) *The State We're In*. London: Jonathan Cape.

Hutton, W (1996) Fools' gold in a fools' paradise. *Observer*, June 2nd.

Pimlott, B & McGregor S (Eds) (1991) *Tackling the Inner City*. London: Clarendon Press.

Pond, C & Burgles, L (1996) The rising tide of deprivation. *New Society*, April 18th.

Class

Bell, C (1968) *Middle Class Families*. London: Routledge & Kegan Paul.

Clarke, J et al. (1979) *Working Class Culture*. London: Hutchinson.

Crompton, R & Jones, G (1984) *White Collar Proletariat*. London: Macmillan.

Halsey, A et al. (1980) *Origins and Destinations*. Oxford: Clarendon Press.

Hutton, W (1995) *The State We're In*. London: Jonathan Cape.

Jamble, A (1985) *Britain in Decline* (2nd edn). London: Methuen.

Leys, C (1983) *Politics in Britain*. London: Heinemann.

Sivanandan, A (1982) *A Different Hunger*. London: Pluto Press.

Politics

Hall, S & Jacques, M (Eds) (1983) *The Politics of Thatcherism*. London: Lawrence & Wishart.

Hare, D (1993) *Asking Around*. London: Faber.

Hefferman, R & Margusee, M (1992) *Defeat from the Jaws of Victory*. London: Verso.

Jenkins, S (1995) *Accountable to None*. London: Penguin.

Kavanage, D (1990) *Thatcherism and British Politics.* London: Clarendon Press.

Miliband, R (1982) *Capitalist Democracy in Britain.* New York: Oxford University Press.

Moodley, R, Lago, C & Talahite, A (2004) *Carl Rogers Counsels a Black Client: Race and culture in person-centred counselling.* Ross-on-Wye: PCCS Books.

Orbach, S (1994) *What's Really Going On Here?* London: Virago.

Proctor, G & Napier MB (Eds) (2004) *Encountering Feminism: Intersections between feminism and the person-centred approach.* Ross-on-Wye: PCCS Books.

Proctor, G, Cooper, M, Sanders, P & Malcolm, B (Eds) (2006) *Politicizing the Person-Centred Approach: An agenda for social change.* Ross-on-Wye: PCCS Books.

Short, J (1996) *The Urban Order.* Oxford: Blackwells.

Young, H (1991) *One of Us.* London: Macmillan.

Counselling

I am assuming that readers will be familiar with the counselling literature, at least enough to access books on counselling in general. As far as ethics and the regulation of counselling are concerned, I would direct the reader to:

British Association for Counselling and Pschotherapy, BACP House, 15 St John's Business Park, Lutterworth LE17 4 HB. Tel: 0870 443 5252. Website: www.bacp.co.uk.

The website contains sections on ethical framework, accreditation, registration, and much more, with downloadable files.

For comments on professionalism and registration in counselling and psychotherapy:

Bates, Y & House, R (2003) *Ethically Challenged Professions: Enabling innovation and diversity in psychotherapy and counselling.* Ross-on-Wye: PCCS Books.

House, R & Totton, N (1997) *Implausible Professions: Arguments for pluralism and autonomy in psychotherapy and counselling.* Ross-on-Wye: PCCS Books.

Mowbray, R (1995) *The Case against Psychotherapy Registration: A conservation issue for the Human Potential Movement.* London: Trnasmarginal Press.

Postle, D (2007) *Regulating the Psychological Therapies.* Ross-on-Wye: PCCS Books.

Thorne, B (1992) Psychotherapy and counselling: The quest for differences. *Counselling. 3*(4), December.

Thorne, B (1995) The accountable therapist. *Self & Society, 23*(4).

Index